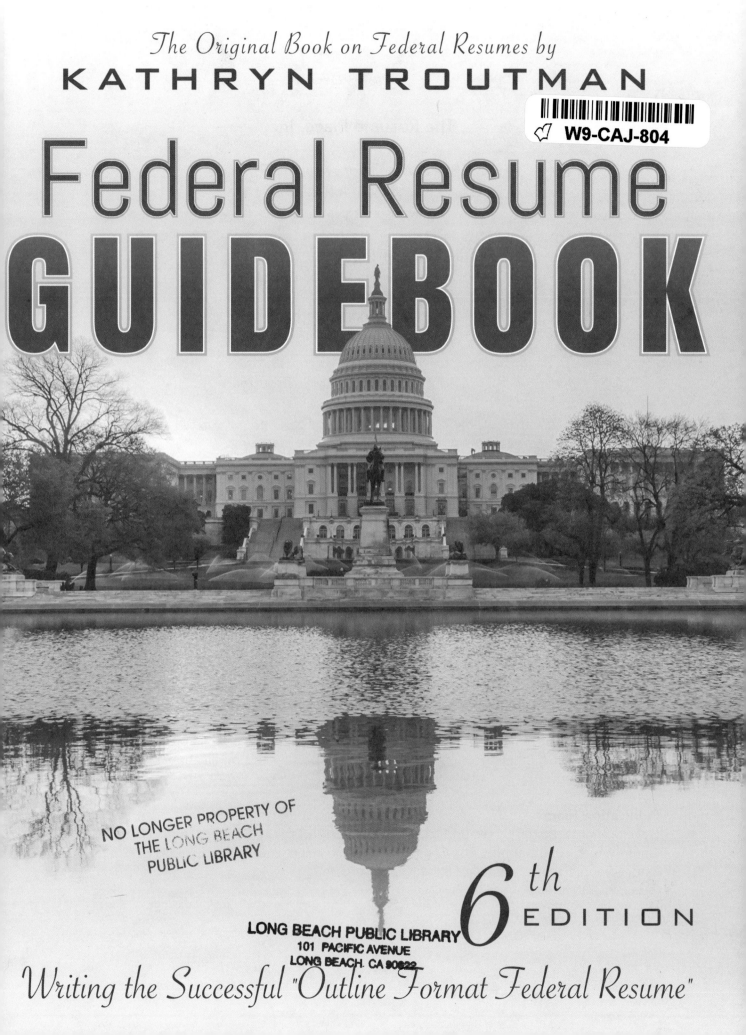

The Original Book on Federal Resumes by

KATHRYN TROUTMAN

Federal Resume
GUIDEBOOK

6th EDITION

Writing the Successful "Outline Format Federal Resume"

The Resume Place, Inc.

P.O. Box 21275, Catonsville, MD 21228
Phone: 888-480-8265
www.resume-place.com

Printed in the United States of America
Federal Resume Guidebook 6th Edition
ISBN-13: 978-0-9861421-2-3
ISBN-10: 0986142123
Updated January 2016

We have been careful to provide accurate federal job search information in this book, but it is possible that errors and omissions may have been introduced.

Sample Resumes: Sample resumes are real but fictionalized. All federal applicants have given permission for their resumes to be used as samples for this publication. Privacy policy is strictly enforced.

Publication Team
Developmental Editor, Cover, and Interior Page Design/Layout: Paulina Chen
Contributors: John Gagnon, Rita Chambers, Debbie Hahn, and Rachel Blazucki
Copyediting: Pamela Sikora and Sarah Greenberg
Index: Pilar Wyman

Table of Contents

Sample Federal Resumes

Introduction by **Kathryn Troutman**

I wrote the first-ever book on Federal Resume Writing, The Federal Resume Guidebook, in 1996 after the government eliminated the SF-171 (sometimes a 50-page form with a table of contents). Ever since the first book, I have been teaching federal job applicants how to write the best federal resume format, from paper format (sometimes 10 to 14 pages) to Resumix format, and now the USAJOBS format (average length of 5 pages).

This latest edition is simpler and shorter, and makes it easier to understand the critical elements of a Best Qualified federal resume. The USAJOBS vacancy announcements are better than ever—really. The job announcements include the keywords and keys to your success with your federal resume. If you REALLY want a federal job, you will follow this guidebook's lessons, samples, and outline format style guide (in the USAJOBS builder) for your federal resume.
At The Resume Place, Inc. we write our federal resumes in this format and we receive many testimonials back from our clients:

> "Looks like our hard work paid off! Interview is scheduled for
> this Friday. Thanks so much! We did one resume for one position,
> a GS-12 with the VA."

The outline format, keywords, accomplishments, and specialized experience hit the mark—Bullseye! We will now prepare for the Behavior-Based Interview!

The bottom line with your federal resume is this:

Your federal resume must demonstrate that you have One Year Specialized Experience at the next lower grade level, and that you have the Knowledge, Skills, and Abilities to perform the position. Your federal resume must also be in the USAJOBS format and cover the KSAs in the resume from the announcement.

Good luck with your federal job search and federal resume! I hope you get Best Qualified, Referred, Interviewed and HIRED into a career ladder position!

Kathryn Troutman
Author and Publisher, *Federal Resume Guidebook, 6th Ed.*

STRATEGY 1 Use the Outline Format

The federal resume is the most important document you can write to support your entrance into federal service, or to obtain a promotion to a new position.

... Private Industry Resume

WHY: Too short. Not enough info.

... Functional Resume

WHY: You must list your most recent employment first, not last.

... Big Block Resume

WHY: Have you tried to actually read one of these lately? It's nearly impossible!

... Bulleted Resume

WHY: This format is usually just another version of the Private Industry resume. Even with bullets, it is still too short and does not have enough detail.

If you ever receive a message like the one below in response to an application, it is time to fix your federal resume format!

"Your resume did not document either the number of hours worked per week for all jobs listed, a detailed description of your duties performed, or the month/year to month/year worked for all jobs listed, as required by the vacancy announcement. Please be sure to read each announcement for complete qualification requirements and instructions on 'How to Apply'."

What Is A **Competitive Federal Resume?**

3 to 5 Pages in Length
WHY: The federal resume must include certain information in order for you to be rated as Best Qualified for a position. Each generalized and specialized skill that you have developed in your career has to be written into the document.

Matches the Job Announcement
WHY: To be successful, the federal resume must match the job announcement by making sure KEYWORDS are very easy to find and showing how how you have the Knowledge Skills, and Abilities for the job, including those listed in the Questionnaire that is Part 2 of the federal job application.

Includes Accomplishments
WHY: In order to be rated Best Qualified, you must include accomplishments demonstrating excellent past performance.

Lists Employment in Reverse Chronological Order
WHY: This order is used by the resume builder in USAJOBS.gov. Refer to the USAJOBS builder to make sure your federal resume includes the required information.

Includes Information Required in Your Federal Resume:
The federal resume **must match** the USAJOBS Resume Builder fields. We recomend that you use the USAJOBS Resume Builder to create your resume for the first time.

- ❯ Month and year of each job you held for at least the last ten years
- ❯ Supervisor names and phone numbers (if they are available)
- ❯ Street addresses, city, state, and zip code of employers for at least 10 years
- ❯ Education with hours completed
- ❯ Majors and colleges with city, state, and zip code
- ❯ Training with titles, sponsoring organizations and classroom hours

And last but not least...
Uses the Outline Format!

USAJOBS resumes are read by <u>Human</u> Resources Specialists – not by an Automated System.

The Outline Format was developed by Kathryn Troutman in the first edition of the *Federal Resume Guidebook* in 1996 and is the preferred format by Human Resources Specialists for readability!

Coastal Development Services
3704 Pacific Avenue, Suite 100
Virginia Beach, VA   23451 United States

11/2015 – Present
Salary: 45,000 USD Per Year
Hours per week: 40
General Clerk III

Duties, Accomplishments and Related Skills:
PAY ADMINISTRATION: Maintain officer and enlisted military pay accounts for 3,708 personnel assigned to supported commands and activities per pertinent directives. Provide information and advice to military customers on all pay, electronic service record entries, dependency data guidelines/updates, and benefits/entitlements.

Paragraphs, not bullets

INVESTIGATIONS AND PROBLEM-SOLVING: Investigate issues and maintain knowledge on the current Military Personnel Manual, Command Pass Coordinator Manual and all other Department of Defense instructions. Analyze military records for discrepancies and deficiencies.

EDUCATION SERVICES, CONSULTATION, AND TRAINING: Provide one-on-one consulting and training. Effectively counseled 290 personnel on education and training opportunities. Properly ordered and prepared advancement worksheets, and administered Navy-wide advancement examinations with zero (0) discrepancies. Approved 57 tuition assistance requests for personnel furthering higher education.

ALL CAPS headlines for each paragraph using KEYWORDS from the announcement

DATA, RECORDS, AND SYSTEMS MANAGEMENT: Provide clerical support and data entry. Operate automated systems to maintain and update electronic records. Prepare transactions by utilizing current pay/personnel input systems to report pay actions as outlined in Department of Defense guidelines and directives. Provide pay and personnel services to Navy personnel utilizing TOPS, NSIPS, and MMPA systems with the uppermost attention to detail. Perform computerized data entry and information processing. Maintain records in a filing system to arrange records in an orderly manner.

Add your accomplishments at the end of each job block

KEY ACCOMPLISHMENTS: Successfully determined the legal and appropriate eligibility of pay entitlements. Commended for ability to operate computerized programs and databases in order to enter, modify, and retrieve sensitive information into and from electronic service records and or reports in a timely and accurate manner. Recognized for effectively processing all required documents for seven (7) personnel advancing through the Command Advancement Program.

What to Include in **Your Federal Resume**

Personal Information

❯ Full name, mailing address (with zip code), day and evening phone numbers (with area codes), and email address (one that you can access outside work if necessary)

Work Experience

Give the following information for your paid and nonpaid work experience related to the job you are applying for (do not send job descriptions):

❯ Job title (include series and grade if it was a federal job)

❯ Duties and accomplishments

❯ Employer's name and specific address, city, state, and zip code

❯ Supervisor's name and phone number (if you have this)

❯ Starting and ending dates (month and year)

❯ Hours per week

❯ Salary (optional, not required)

❯ Indicate whether you give permission to contact your current supervisor (saying "no" is acceptable and will not affect your chances of being considered for the position)

Education

❯ Colleges or universities

❯ Name, city, and state (zip code)

❯ Majors

❯ Type and year of any degrees received (if no degree, show total credits earned and indicate whether semester or quarter hours)

❯ Copy of your college transcript (only if the job vacancy announcement requests it), upload in USAJOBS account

Other Qualifications

❯ Job-related training courses (title and year/classroom hours and certificate if you received this)

❯ Job-related skills; for example, other languages, computer software/hardware, tools, machinery, and typing speed

❯ Job-related certificates and licenses (current only)

❯ Job-related honors, awards, and special accomplishments; for example, publications, memberships in professional or honor societies, leadership activities, public speaking, and performance awards (give dates but do not send documents unless requested)

This information is listed in the OPM OF-510, *Applying for a Federal Job*
www.gpo.gov/pdfs/careers/apply/of0510.pdf

Before and After **Federal Resumes**

On the following pages, we'll show you four examples of before and after federal resumes. Each before example will have at least one of the three resume versions:

BEFORE: Big Block Resume

The Big Block resume was popular during the "Resumix" days with the Department of Defense artificial intelligence system. The Resumix system was retired in 2010, and now the DOD agencies are using USAJOBS. The Resumix system was initially read by a machine for keywords and the big block could be used, but now USAJOBS resumes are read by staffing specialists. They do NOT like to read a big block of words.

BEFORE: Bulleted Resume

The bullet laundry list resume is not recommended because the specialized experience and Knowledge, Skills and Abilities are too difficult to find in a long list of bullets. A five-page resume with bullets could include as many as 400 bullets!

BEFORE: Functional Resume

The functional resume will not work for a government application, because the duties and responsibilities are not anchored with dates, locations, and job titles. You must show that you have "one year specialized experience" in a certain field of work. Also, if the duties are separated from the dates, you will become ineligible.

AFTER: Outline Format Resume

The Outline Format is preferred by staffing specialists, because it is easy to read and features keywords and accomplishments. Each paragraph represents a skill set that the job announcement requires. The Knowledge, Skills, and Abilities that are required to get Best Qualified for the position are clearly demonstrated in the resume. Every word in the Outline Format is carefully selected to match the job announcement and highlight the person's employment experience and competencies.

STRATEGY **1** : Use the Outline Format

TSA Lead Screener, Pay Band I, Targeting Pay Band J
BEFORE: BIG BLOCK RESUME

See how the big block resume is hard to read!

PROFESSIONAL EXPERIENCE
10/2012–Present: Lead Transportation Security Inspector-Aviation, SV-1801-I, Transportation Security Administration, Compliance Division, Department of Homeland Security, City, State. $75,551.00/year; 40 hours/week; Supervisor: Director Name, 444-666-1111. Permission to contact.

Principal advisor to leadership relative to the applicable security programs/TSA security directives and requirements. Assess impact of management decisions on daily operations. Report courses of action to management in a concise, professional, and unbiased manner. Conduct cost/benefit analysis to ensure appropriateness of recommendations. Serve as Acting Assistant Federal Security Director on multiple occasions when Assistant Federal Security Director is detailed to other locations. Managed seamless transition of duties for a 3-month period while Assistant Director was detailed to headquarters with no disruption in operations. Evaluate mission-critical programs and operational requirements. Identify and evaluate underlying causes of issues; distinguish relevant from irrelevant information; weigh alternative solutions in advance of deadlines with limited guidance. Conduct risk analysis and develop specific contingency plans to overcome risks. Team Lead for Aviation Inspectors. Am role model and peer-to-peer coach. Consistently volunteer services, on short notice, to meet unexpected challenges and circumstances. Engage team and subordinates in project planning and tasking; gain project buy-in through involvement. Ensure understanding of mission and objectives; troubleshoot problems to develop solutions. Implement TSA's SOPs and Security Directives to conduct inspections. Adhere to directives/policies in making decisions; recognize implications of decisions relative to laws and regulations. Substantial knowledge of Title 49 Code of Federal Regulations, TSA National Investigation and Enforcement Manual Procedures, and TSI Handbook. Investigate security concerns; establish preventative methods/procedures. Support safe execution of large public events. Train screeners and personnel in new No Fly and Selectee lists, including knowledge of the laws and regulations, and training in communicating with potential No Fly passengers. Developed the Transportation Security Inspector on-the-job training program.

BEFORE: BULLETED RESUME

It's too hard to find the relevant skills in this format.

PROFESSIONAL EXPERIENCE

10/2012–Present: Lead Transportation Security Inspector-Aviation, SV-1801-I, Transportation Security Administration, Compliance Division, Department of Homeland Security, City, State. $75,551.00/year; 40 hours/week; Supervisor: Director Name, 444-666-1111. Permission to contact.

- Assess impact of management decisions on daily operations.
- Report courses of action to management in a concise, professional, and unbiased manner.
- Conduct cost/benefit analysis to ensure appropriateness of recommendations.
- Managed seamless transition of duties for a 3-month period while Assistant Director was detailed to headquarters with no disruption in operations.
- Identify and evaluate underlying causes of issues; distinguish relevant from irrelevant information; weigh alternative solutions in advance of deadlines with limited guidance. Conduct RISK ANALYSIS and develop specific contingency plans to overcome risks.
- Engage team and subordinates in project planning and tasking; gain project buy-in through involvement. Ensure understanding of mission and objectives; troubleshoot problems to develop solutions.
- Adhere to directives/policies in making decisions; recognize implications of decisions relative to laws and regulations.
- Substantial knowledge of Title 49 Code of Federal Regulations, TSA National Investigation and Enforcement Manual Procedures, and TSI Handbook.
- Investigate security concerns; establish preventative methods/procedures.
- Train screeners and personnel in new No Fly and Selectee lists, including knowledge of the laws and regulations, and training in communicating with potential No Fly passengers.
- Developed the Transportation Security Inspector on-the-job training program. .
- I successfully managed the access security program, evaluated performance improvements, and ensured compliance with laws and regulations. RESULT: The airport achieved gateway approval in early June 2012. Flights began shortly afterwards. I received a time-off award for superlative work
- Co-managed a tense situation with a No Fly passenger who was on the list in error. Was able to resolve the problem without the passenger missing the flight, but also ensuring a safe and secure flight.

TSA Lead Screener, Pay Band I, Targeting Pay Band J
AFTER: OUTLINE FORMAT RESUME

Keywords and accomplishments stand out!

PROFESSIONAL EXPERIENCE

10/2012–Present: Lead Transportation Security Inspector-Aviation, SV-1801-I, Transportation Security Administration, Compliance Division, Department of Homeland Security, City, State. $75,551.00/year; 40 hours/week; Supervisor: Director Name, 444-666-1111. Permission to contact.

PRINCIPAL ADVISOR to leadership relative to the applicable security programs/TSA security directives and requirements. Assess impact of management decisions on daily operations. Report courses of action to management in a concise, professional, and unbiased manner. Conduct cost/benefit analysis to ensure appropriateness of recommendations.

Serve as ACTING ASSISTANT FEDERAL SECURITY DIRECTOR on multiple occasions when Assistant Federal Security Director is detailed to other locations. Managed seamless transition of duties for a 3-month period while Assistant Director was detailed to headquarters with no disruption in operations.

SOLVE COMPLEX SECURITY PROBLEMS: Apply experience and comprehensive technical knowledge and understanding of new technologies and methodologies. Evaluate mission-critical programs and operational requirements. Identify and evaluate underlying causes of issues; distinguish relevant from irrelevant information; weigh alternative solutions in advance of deadlines with limited guidance. Conduct RISK ANALYSIS and develop specific contingency plans to overcome risks.

LEADER/PROGRAM MANAGER for Ronald Reagan Washington National Airport (DCA) Access Security Program (DASSP) to support new designation of local airport as a Gateway Airport. My work put planes in the air.

LEAD TEAMS/SUPERVISE STAFF as Team Lead for Aviation Inspectors. Am role model and peer-to-peer coach. Consistently volunteer services, on short notice, to meet unexpected challenges and circumstances. CONFLICT MANAGEMENT: Engage team and subordinates in project planning and tasking; gain project buy-in through involvement. Ensure understanding of mission and objectives; troubleshoot problems to develop solutions.

APPLY KNOWLEDGE OF LAWS/POLICIES/DIRECTIVES: Implement TSA's SOPs and Security Directives to conduct inspections. Adhere to directives/policies in making decisions; recognize implications of decisions relative to laws and regulations. Substantial knowledge of Title 49 Code of Federal Regulations, TSA National Investigation and Enforcement Manual Procedures, and TSI Handbook.

INDEPENDENTLY CONDUCT INSPECTION/COMPLIANCE ASSESSMENTS. Investigate security concerns; establish preventative methods/procedures.

CONDUCT VULNERABILITY ASSESSMENTS to test effectiveness of airports' current security systems and procedures. Support safe execution of large public events.

Execute SPECIAL EMPHASIS INSPECTION (SEI) as directed by headquarters. Train screeners and personnel in new No Fly and Selectee lists, including knowledge of the laws and regulations, and training in communicating with potential No Fly passengers.

PROVIDE TRAINING to new inspectors. Developed the Transportation Security Inspector on-the-job training program.

KEY ACCOMPLISHMENTS:

- During a championship tournament, which brought a large number of visitors and high-profile VIPs to the local county airport, I liaised with tournament planner concerning schedule in order to plan and alert screeners of heavy flight activities and equipment being carried on board. Resolved a major significant golf bag problem that required hand carrying, due to late flight for a significant tournament deadline. Recognized for outstanding customer services by top golf pro in the country.

- My ingenuity boosted gateway security and resolved a dispute with a carrier. The carrier was facing fines for gateway violations. I negotiated with the carrier and convinced it to commit to reasonable security improvements instead of paying fines. RESULT: No security violations from this carrier since implementing my solution.

- I encouraged local corporate flight departments and the local fixed-base operator to cooperate. I successfully managed the access security program, evaluated performance improvements, and ensured compliance with laws and regulations. RESULT: The airport achieved gateway approval in early June 2012. Flights began shortly afterwards. I received a time-off award for superlative work

- I maximize my team's performance and let individuals shine. When one individual was faltering, I mentored that individual, ensured tasks were equally distributed, and specifically deleted tasks to keep projects on schedule. RESULT: I have created an inclusive environment, motivated the staff, and improved overall performance. The staff has provided positive feedback about my inspections.

Legal Collections Analyst, GS-0408-11
BEFORE: BIG BLOCK RESUME

STRATEGY **1** : Use the Outline Format

See how the big block resume is hard to read!

Legal Collections Analyst II   04/2014 – Present
Judicial Collections Analyst I
Division Enterprise Equity Services

Prepare legal documents for debt collection, such as affidavits and responses to discovery requests, by using automated software. Review legal documents, such as complaints, pleadings and judgments, and various other legal documents to ensure figures and facts are correct. Produce reports and documents on legal matters regarding debt collection accounts along with written correspondence with attorneys and parties involved in the debt collection file.. Monitor the progress of litigation and make recommendations to continue pursuit of cases. For example, I may review legal arguments from debtors and determine if their argument would hinder the ability to attain a judgment or analyze a judge who may have a tendency to be debtor friendly. Negotiate settlements with debtors on collection files to achieve the highest collection total possible in over 400 debt collection accounts. Speak with debtors to work towards a settlement agreement, either through a lump sum or a payment schedule. Review financial information of the debtors, such as filed tax returns, bank statements, pay stubs, and other asset searches, to determine the current and future ability to repay the debt and attempt to persuade debtors to reach a mutually acceptable settlement. Provide recommendations to management on complex settlement accounts. Review state statutes and case law to determine best approaches in attaining a judgment in court and to best counter legal arguments from debtors. Provide information or assistance and attempt to resolve issues ranging from negotiating settlements, explaining the details how my company came to acquire the mortgage loan, and discussing strategy with attorneys to resolve legal arguments from defendants. Manage assigned case files in coordination with a network of 16 law firms outside of my company to make certain files are up to date. Utilize excellent communication skills to prepare formal written correspondence along with effective telephonic communication to convey instructions to law firms on how to proceed with accounts. Correspond with various office personnel, ranging from attorneys to support staff. Document all interaction and notate the information into the electronic database system called AdvantEdge CS (ADS). Ensure files are within the statute of limitations to file a debt collections lawsuit along with verifying the total amount sued upon is correct and accurate. Review all collection file notes and documents to make sure all the documentation, most notably the note, mortgage, and the assignments, are correct. Upper management set a department goal of $3.60 million for total collections and my department exceeded the goal by collecting $4.08 million. I was able to collect $1.13 million solely through my accounts. Create and analyze debtor financial profiles by reviewing the debtor's place of employment, tax returns, credit bureau report, potential for filing bankruptcy, and other details to determine the collectability of the file. Excellent personal computer skills in developing and utilizing spreadsheets, databases, and professional documents to improve operational readiness, manage and organize files, and research information. Excellent utilization of computer software, such as Microsoft Office (Excel, Word, and Outlook) and an electronic account database; exceptional handling of office equipment, for instance, fax machines, copiers, scanners, printers, and multi-line telephone systems.

BEFORE: BULLETED RESUME

It's too hard to find the relevant skills in this format.

Legal Collections Analyst II   04/2014 – Present
Judicial Collections Analyst I
Division Enterprise Equity Services

- Responsible for preparing legal documents for debt collection litigation, such as affidavits and responses to discovery requests, by using automated software.
- Participate in reviewing legal documents, such as complaints, pleadings and judgments, and various other legal documents to ensure figures and facts are correct.
- Additional duties include producing reports and documents on legal matters regarding debt collection accounts along with written correspondence with attorneys and parties involved in the debt collection file.
- Help with analyzing applicable federal and state statutes along with case law and legal precedent to further determine collectability of an account in litigation.
- Participate in the progress of litigation and make recommendations to continue pursuit of cases.
- Collaborate on reviewing legal arguments from debtors and determine if their argument would hinder the ability to attain a judgment or analyze a judge who may have a tendency to be debtor friendly.
- Help with case coordination for our network of 16 law firms outside of my company to make certain files are up to date.
- Responsible for negotiating settlements with debtors on collection files to achieve the highest collection total possible in over 400 debt collection accounts.
- On occasion, speak with debtors to work towards a settlement agreement, either through a lump sum or a payment schedule.
- Provide support for the review financial information of the debtors, such as filed tax returns, bank statements, pay stubs, and other asset searches, to determine the current and future ability to repay the debt and attempt to persuade debtors to reach a mutually acceptable settlement. Provide recommendations to management on complex settlement accounts.
- Other duties include: Reviewing state statutes and case law to determine best approaches in attaining a judgment in court and to best counter legal arguments from debtors; ensuring all accounts are in compliance with the Fair Debt Collection Practices Act (FDCPA) and making sure all collection methods are being used, including writ of execution, wage garnishment, bank garnishment, and placing liens on all real property; assisting with negotiating settlements, explaining the details how my company came to acquire the mortgage loan; and discussing strategy with attorneys to resolve legal arguments from defendants.
- Helped to achieve a record collection totals in my department in the year of 2014 and also surpassed the collection total goal set by upper management. Upper management set a department goal of $3.60 million for total collections and my department exceeded the goal by collecting $4.08 million. I was able to collect $1.13 million solely through my accounts.

Before & After Samples: **Legal Assistant**

Legal Collections Analyst, GS-0408-11

AFTER: OUTLINE FORMAT RESUME

Keywords and accomplishments stand out!

Legal Collections Analyst II   04/2014 –
Present
Division Enterprise Equity Services   40 Hours per
week
3000 Henninger Road $41,437 per
Year
St. Paul, MN 90999

Supervisor: Buddy Que, Judicial Collections Manager
May not be contacted: Phone Number - (888) 888-8888

PREPARE LEGAL DOCUMENTS FOR DEBT COLLECTION LITIGATION, such as affidavits and responses to discovery requests, by using automated software. Review legal documents, such as complaints, pleadings and judgments, and various other legal documents to ensure figures and facts are correct. Produce reports and documents on legal matters regarding debt collection accounts along with written correspondence with attorneys and parties involved in the debt collection file.

REVIEW AND APPLY KNOWLEDGE OF LAWS associated with debt collection. Analyze applicable federal and state statutes along with case law and legal precedent to further determine collectability of an account in litigation. Monitor the progress of litigation and make recommendations to continue pursuit of cases. For example, I may review legal arguments from debtors and determine if their argument would hinder the ability to attain a judgment or analyze a judge who may have a tendency to be debtor friendly.

NEGOTIATE SETTLEMENTS WITH DEBTORS ON COLLECTION FILES to achieve the highest collection total possible in over 400 debt collection accounts. Speak with debtors to work towards a settlement agreement, either through a lump sum or a payment schedule. Review financial information of the debtors, such as filed tax returns, bank statements, pay stubs, and other asset searches, to determine the current and future ability to repay the debt and attempt to persuade debtors to reach a mutually acceptable settlement. Provide recommendations to management on complex settlement accounts.

UTILIZE EXCELLENT TECHNICAL COMPETENCE IN DEBT COLLECTION to achieve high collection results. Review state statutes and case law to determine best approaches in attaining a judgment in court and to best counter legal arguments from debtors. Ensure all accounts are in compliance with the Fair Debt Collection Practices Act (FDCPA) and make sure all collection methods are being used, including writ of execution, wage garnishment, bank garnishment, and placing liens on all real property.

EXERCISE EXCEPTIONAL CUSTOMER SERVICE AND EXCELLENT COMMUNICATION SKILLS while dealing with a variety of individuals to resolve issues in debt collection files. Individuals range from debtors and defendants, attorneys, office personnel, members of the Court, debt counseling agencies, mediators, and others. Provide information or assistance and attempt to resolve issues ranging from negotiating settlements, explaining the details how my company came to acquire the mortgage loan, and discussing strategy with attorneys to resolve legal arguments from defendants.

MANAGE AND WORK ASSIGNED CASE FILES in coordination with a network of 16 law firms outside of my company to make certain files are up to date. Utilize excellent communication skills to prepare formal written correspondence along with effective telephonic communication to convey instructions to law firms on how to proceed with accounts. Correspond with various office personnel, ranging from attorneys to support staff. Document all interaction and notate the information into the electronic database system called AdvantEdge CS (ADS).

REVIEW AND ANALYZE DEBT COLLECTION ACCOUNTS FOR LEGAL MERIT AND COMPLIANCE with the Fair Debt Collection Practices Act (FDCPA). Ensure files are within the statute of limitations to file a debt collections lawsuit along with verifying the total amount sued upon is correct and accurate. Review all collection file notes and documents to make sure all the documentation, most notably the note, mortgage, and the assignments, are correct. Analyze the account to determine the type of indebtedness, such as a purchase money loan or a refinance loan.

MAKE RECOMMENDATIONS AND TAKE APPROPRIATE LEGAL ACTION through determining the cost effectiveness of pursuing debtors in debt collection litigation. Create and analyze debtor financial profiles by reviewing the debtor's place of employment, tax returns, credit bureau report, potential for filing bankruptcy, and other details to determine the collectability of the file.

USE OFFICE AUTOMATION to prepare, analyze, organize, and process reports and data. Excellent personal computer skills in developing and utilizing spreadsheets, databases, and professional documents to improve operational readiness, manage and organize files, and research information. Excellent utilization of computer software, such as Microsoft Office (Excel, Word, and Outlook) and an electronic account database; exceptional handling of office equipment, such as fax machines, copiers, scanners, printers, and multi-line telephone systems.

KEY ACCOMPLISHMENTS

+ Achieved record collection totals in my department in the year of 2014 and also surpassed the collection total goal set by upper management. Upper management set a department goal of $3.60 million for total collections and my department exceeded the goal by collecting $4.08 million. I was able to collect $1.13 million solely through my accounts.

+ I took on the task of revamping the inner dynamics of my department and changed outdated procedures that encumbered the department from achieving high results. Reviewed all accounts, over 1,200 over three months, to determine eligibility for collections and set higher standards for the law firms that represented my company to push for better collection efforts. I constantly and daily maintain accounts to ensure they are up to date.

Before & After Samples: **Program Analyst**

Inventory & Monitoring Program Analyst, GS-13, targeting GS-13

BEFORE: BIG BLOCK RESUME

See how the big block resume is hard to read!

MANAGEMENT AND PROGRAM ANALYST, GS-0343-13
Commander, Navy Installations Command
Washington Navy Yard, Washington, DC
Supervisor and phone

02/2011 to 07/2014
40 Hours per Week

Transient Personnel Branch, Military Personnel Services (MILPERS), Navy Installations Command, Entitlement Travel, and Navy Mobilization Sites. Managed financial and civilian and military manpower resources for all US Navy Pay Transient Personnel Units (TPUs) and Shore Corrections (Regional Restricted Barracks, Pretrial Confinement Facilities) (PCFs) and Detention Facilities (DETFACs), worldwide. Leveraged technical expertise and strong leadership and project management skills; and expert knowledge of CNIC and its business/support lines to plan, program, budget, and execute TPU operations and Shore Corrections, worldwide. Developed and monitored program execution consistent with the CNIC Strategic Plan. Ensured effective management and standardization of Navy-wide resources and business processes across the shore installation network. Identified and validated requirements. Managed rapid, ready, professional manpower support to mobilized and demobilized Active and Reserve Components called in support of contingency operations worldwide; with a primary focus on Afghanistan, Iraq and Horn of Africa. Planned and managed a $6M+ annual program budget for the Transient Personnel Branch. Develop estimates for labor, non-labor: training, travel, supplies, and contracts. Wrote contract solicitation, statements of work (SOWs), and review proposals. Submit Total Force Manpower Management packages to change billet description and reassign manpower throughout the enterprise. Created an annual spend plan for labor and non-labor, track program execution rates, notify leadership of budget shortfalls and justify funding for critical shortfalls. Managed a $2.5M Entitlement Travel Program budget with a statutory requirement to pay for military and civilian personnel and their dependents assigned overseas for Emergency and Funded Environmental Morale leave; Travel for Medical Escorts and Attendants and Medical Travel; and Student Dependent Travel. Manage four government contracts in access of $1.9 million. N1 Total Force Manpower Technical Expert assigned to review proposals and make selection recommendation to Contracting Officer. Submit contracting packages for sole source funding, execution of option year, and write Statement of Work for new solicitations. Ensure all contracting solicitations are complete, accurate, and compliant. Ensure accuracy of monthly funding execution; approve invoice payments. Work directly with vendors to rectify discrepancies. Also serve as Contractor Verification System (CVS) representative for N1. Ensure initial security clearance processing for all contractors joining the CNIC N1 Total Force Management Team. Provided the Navy with a standardized and consolidated platform that will minimize the average time a Sailor spends in any given transient processing category. The new system was successfully rolled out in 6/2012 and is operational at all seven TPU's and five TPD's. Navy leadership can now track performance metrics for 20,000 transients being processed across the TPU Enterprise. It features a customized dashboard, which allows CNIC leadership to engage external stakeholders to mitigate the opportunity costs associated with TPU processing.

It's too hard to find the relevant skills in this format.

MANAGEMENT AND PROGRAM ANALYST, GS-0343-13
Commander, Navy Installations Command
Washington Navy Yard, Washington, DC
Supervisor and phone

02/2011 to 07/2014
40 Hours per Week

- Transient Personnel Branch, Military Personnel Services (MILPERS), Navy Installations Command, Entitlement Travel, and Navy Mobilization Sites.
- Managed financial and civilian and military manpower resources for all US Navy Pay Transient Personnel Units (TPUs) and Shore Corrections (Regional Restricted Barracks, Pretrial Confinement Facilities) (PCFs) and Detention Facilities (DETFACs), worldwide.
- Leveraged technical expertise and strong leadership and project management skills; and expert knowledge of CNIC and its business/support lines to plan, program, budget, and execute TPU operations and Shore Corrections, worldwide.
- Developed and monitored program execution consistent with the CNIC Strategic Plan.
- Ensured effective management and standardization of Navy-wide resources and business processes across the shore installation network. Identified and validated requirements.
- Managed rapid, ready, professional manpower support to mobilized and demobilized Active and Reserve Components called in support of contingency operations worldwide; with a primary focus on Afghanistan, Iraq and Horn of Africa.
- Planned and managed a $6M+ annual program budget for the Transient Personnel Branch.
- Develop estimates for labor, non-labor: training, travel, supplies, and contracts. Wrote contract solicitation, statements of work (SOWs), and review proposals.
- Submit Total Force Manpower Management packages to change billet description and reassign manpower throughout the enterprise. Created an annual spend plan for labor and non-labor, track program execution rates, notify leadership of budget shortfalls and justify funding for critical shortfalls.
- Managed a $2.5M Entitlement Travel Program budget with a statutory requirement to pay for military and civilian personnel and their dependents assigned overseas for Emergency and Funded Environmental Morale leave; Travel for Medical Escorts and Attendants and Medical Travel; and Student Dependent Travel.
- Manage four government contracts in access of $1.9 million. N1 Total Force Manpower Technical Expert assigned to review proposals and make selection recommendation to Contracting Officer.
- Submit contracting packages for sole source funding, execution of option year, and write Statement of Work for new solicitations.

Before & After Samples: **Program Analyst**

Inventory & Monitoring Program Analyst, GS-13, targeting GS-14

AFTER: OUTLINE FORMAT RESUME

Keywords and accomplishments stand out!

MANAGEMENT AND PROGRAM ANALYST, GS-0343-13	02/2011 to 07/2014
Commander, Navy Installations Command	40 Hours per Week
Washington Navy Yard, Washington, DC	
Supervisor and phone	

PROGRAM AND MANAGEMENT ANALYST: Transient Personnel Branch, Military Personnel Services (MILPERS), Navy Installations Command, Entitlement Travel, and Navy Mobilization Sites. Managed financial and civilian and military manpower resources for all US Navy Pay Transient Personnel Units (TPUs) and Shore Corrections (Regional Restricted Barracks, Pretrial Confinement Facilities [PCFs]) and Detention Facilities worldwide.

RESOURCE MANAGER AND QUALITY ASSURANCE: Leveraged technical expertise and knowledge of business/support lines to plan, program, budget, and execute TPU operations and Shore Corrections, worldwide. Developed and monitored program execution consistent with the CNIC Strategic Plan. Ensured effective management and standardization of Navy-wide resources and business processes across the shore installation network. Identified and validated requirements.

MOBILIZATION PROCESSING SITE MANAGER: Managed rapid, ready, professional manpower support to mobilized and demobilized Active and Reserve Components called in support of contingency operations worldwide, with a primary focus on Afghanistan, Iraq and Horn of Africa.

BUDGET MANAGEMENT: Planned and managed a $6M+ annual program budget for the Transient Personnel Branch. Developed estimates for labor, non-labor: training, travel, supplies, and contracts. Wrote contract solicitation, statements of work (SOWs), and review proposals. Submitted Total Force Manpower Management packages to change billet description and reassign manpower throughout the enterprise. Created an annual spend plan for labor and non-labor, tracked program execution rates, notified leadership of budget shortfalls, and justified funding for critical shortfalls.

TRAVEL BUDGET MANAGER: Managed a $2.5M Entitlement Travel Program budget with a statutory requirement to pay for military and civilian personnel and their dependents assigned overseas for Emergency and Funded Environmental Morale leave; Travel for Medical Escorts and Attendants and Medical Travel; and Student Dependent Travel.

CONTRACT OFFICER REPRESENTATIVE (COR): Managed four government contracts in access of $1.9 million. N1 Total Force Manpower Technical Expert assigned to review proposals and make selection recommendation to Contracting Officer. Submitted contracting packages for sole source funding, execution of option year, and wrote Statement of Work for new solicitations. Ensured all contracting solicitations are complete, accurate, and compliant. Ensure accuracy of monthly funding execution; approve invoice payments. Worked directly with vendors to rectify discrepancies.

KEY ACCOMPLISHMENTS:

- Developed, planned, and implemented the U.S. Navy's first standardized, Web-based Transient Personnel Tracking System (WTPTS SQL Server System), providing the Navy with a standardized and consolidated platform that will minimize the average time a Sailor spends in any given transient processing category. The new system was successfully rolled out in 6/2012 and is operational at all seven TPU's and five TPD's. Navy leadership can now track performance metrics for 20,000 transients being processed across the TPU Enterprise. It features a customized dashboard, which allows CNIC leadership to engage external stakeholders to mitigate the opportunity costs associated with TPU processing.

- Business Case Analysis (BCA): Developed a BCA in 11/2013 to evaluate possible courses of action (COAs) that correlate to USFFC's IA drawdown plan. Led team in data collection to formulate an environmental scan capturing cost information for transportation, berthing, manning (MPN/FTS), supplies, and additional OCO funding. Managed conversion of tangible cost data for each COA into a spreadsheet. Analyzed and developed recommendations. Results: The recommendations I presented were approved by Navy leadership at the 3-star level and implemented for a $5M cost savings over two years. The first facility closure was at NMPS Point Hueneme in June 2012.

- Developed and led process and efficiency improvements and cost savings measures that reduced contracts and manpower costs across the enterprise. Provided mission-critical quantitative and qualitative analysis to support decision-making at the highest levels of the Navy, including initiation of an 8% budget cut. Provided guidance to all regions for more stringent enforcement of entitlement travel expenditures.

IT Specialist, GS-9
BEFORE: FUNCTIONAL RESUME

The job duties and responsibilities are not tied to the dates and job titles!

Summary of Skills:

COMPUTER NETWORK HARDWARE AND COMMUNICATION EQUIPMENT SPECIALIST: Deploy, sustain, troubleshoot, and repair standard voice, data, and video network infrastructure systems, IP detection systems and cryptographic equipment. Perform, coordinate, integrate, and supervise network design, configuration, operation, defense, restoration, and improvements. Analyze capabilities and performance, identify problems, and take corrective action. Fabricate, terminate, and interconnect wiring and associated network infrastructure devices. Apply knowledge obtained from reading and understanding highly technical manuals. Apply extensive knowledge of IT operating systems, applications, and ADP equipment configurations and components.

ESTABLISH AND MANAGE INTERNET GATEWAY COMMUNICATIONS secure IP and voice service (VoIP) within 30 minutes using Theater Deployable Communication (TDC) Integrated Communication Access Package (ICAP). Provide EFFECTIVE, HIGH QUALITY IT CUSTOMER SERVICE and support, including in remote locations, by ensuring reliable customer access to secure and non-secure networks for up to 100 users. Set up and configure REDCOM Basic Access Module telephone switching networks.

COMPLETED OVER 150 COMPUTER HARDWARE and electronic diagnostic checks with zero discrepancies resulting in ship's readiness for deployment. Performed all basic electric maintenance in the CIC. Applied knowledge obtained from reading and understanding highly technical manuals.

Work History:

Maryland Air National Guard (MDNG)
175th Communications Squadron, 175th Wing Martin State Airport Baltimore, MD United States, 11/2014 – Present

CYBER TRANSPORT STAFF SERGEANT
USN, USS Stout Norfolk, VA United States, 07/2011 – 11/2014

OPERATIONS SPECIALIST, E-5
USN, Navy Amphibious Base Little Creek, VA United States, 11/2009 – 07/2011

AFTER: OUTLINE FORMAT RESUME

Each position includes duties, responsibilities, projects, and skills.

Work Experience:

Maryland Air National Guard (MDNG)
175th Communications Squadron, 175th Wing
Martin State Airport, Baltimore, MD   United States
11/2014 - Present
Salary: 2,800.00 USD Per Month
Hours per week: 40

CYBER TRANSPORT STAFF SERGEANT

Duties, Accomplishments and Related Skills:

CYBER TRANSPORT IT SPECIALIST currently serving in MDNG. As a NETWORK TECHNICIAN for the 175th Communications Squadron and the 175th Wing, provide essential IT customer support services for up to 500 staff.

COMPUTER NETWORK HARDWARE AND COMMUNICATION EQUIPMENT SPECIALIST: Deploy, sustain, troubleshoot, and repair standard voice, data, and video network infrastructure systems, IP detection systems and cryptographic equipment. Perform, coordinate, integrate, and supervise network design, configuration, operation, defense, restoration, and improvements. Analyze capabilities and performance, identify problems, and take corrective action. Fabricate, terminate, and interconnect wiring and associated network infrastructure devices. Apply knowledge obtained from reading and understanding highly technical manuals. Apply extensive knowledge of IT operating systems, applications, and ADP equipment configurations and components.

ESTABLISH AND MANAGE INTERNET GATEWAY COMMUNICATIONS: Secure IP and voice service (VoIP) within 30 minutes using Theater Deployable Communication (TDC) Integrated Communication Access Package (ICAP). Provide EFFECTIVE, HIGH QUALITY IT CUSTOMER SERVICE and support, including in remote locations, by ensuring reliable customer access to secure and non-secure networks for up to 100 users.

• Set up and configure REDCOM Basic Access Module telephone switching networks.

• Fabricate and connect category 5 and fiber optic network cables.

• Troubleshoot to diagnose and repair computer network hardware and software problems.

• Install software updates and patches on existing network infrastructure.

• Work closely with supervisor to maintain network security.

STRATEGY 2 How Many Hats Do You Wear at Work?

Team Member   Project Manager   Technician   Instructor   Administrator

em Solver   IT Specialist   Briefer   Mentor   Analyst   Customer Ser

Building the Outline Format federal resume will require that you break up the Work Experience section of the resume into smaller paragraphs that focus on specific skills. We find it helpful to start by thinking about the major hats that we wear at work.

What are the 5 to 7 hats that you wear in your job?

_____

_____

_____

_____

_____

_____

_____

_____

_____

_____

_____

Sample "Hats"

Sample 1:

Shenandoah National Park, Maintenance Mechanic

- Maintenance Mechanic
- Preventative Maintenance
- Communications / Team Work
- Safety and Sanitation Knowledge
- Equipment Skills
- Small Tools
- Problem-solving

National Park Service   05/2015 - Present
3655 US Highway 2011 E
Luray, VA   22835 United States

Maintenance Mechanic
Duties, Accomplishments and Related Skills:

MAINTENANCE MECHANIC - Repair facilities, buildings, and historic structures.
Experienced in carpentry, painting, and roofing to maintain park buildings and facilities.
Performed wood repair and painting for the Hoover Building, Interior and Exterior. Every room
in the property. Exterior, Front Porch and Deck. Ensured paint colors and types of pain to meet
Historic Preservation Requirements.

PREVENTATIVE MAINTENANCE: Preventive and construction maintenance on structures
that require a knowledge of woodworking tools and equipment and historic preservation
methods.

COMMUNICATIONS / TEAM WORK: Communicate with staff concerning repairs, schedule
and maintenance requirements.

COLLABORATE WITH SAFETY AND SANITATION. Coordinate with sanitation group
cleaning comfort stations and buildings throughout the park as needed.

EQUIPMENT SKILLS: Operate 4x4 pickups, small trailers, etc.) to complete work projects.
Perform normal carpentry, painting, and roofing repairs and maintenance such as replacing door
frames, constructing stairways and decks, repair/replace roofs and rafters, etc.

SMALL TOOLS: Your experience included using common tools such as hand saw, table saw,
sander, framing square, chisel, etc.

PROBLEM-SOLVING: Skilled in solving problems with carpentry, maintenance projects.

Sample 2: **Management and Program Analyst, GS-0343-13**

Commander, Navy Installations Command, Washington Navy Yard, Washington, DC

- ❯ Program And Management Analyst
- ❯ Resource Manager And Quality Assurance
- ❯ Mobilization Processing Site Manager
- ❯ Budget Management
- ❯ Travel Budget Manager
- ❯ Contract Officer Representative (COR)

Sample 3: **Ecologist (Interdisciplinary) GS-0408-11**

Inventory & Monitoring (I&M), Pacific Island Network (PACN)

- ❯ Project Manager
- ❯ Contracting Officer's Representative (COR/COTR):
- ❯ Supervisor
- ❯ Safety Officer
- ❯ Liaison

Sample 4: **Lead Transportation Security Inspector-Aviation**

SV-1801-I, Transportation Security Administration

- ❯ Principal Advisor
- ❯ Acting Assistant Federal Security Director
- ❯ Solve Complex Security Problems
- ❯ Team Leader/Leader/Program Manager
- ❯ Apply Knowledge Of Laws/Policies/Directives
- ❯ Independently Conduct Inspection/Compliance Assessments
- ❯ Conduct Vulnerability Assessments

Sample 5: **Quality Assurance Specialist, WG-0861-10**

Tobyhanna Army Depot, Tobyhanna, Pennsylvania

- ❯ Metal Foreman / Project Planner
- ❯ Team Member
- ❯ Trainer / Mentor / Safety Trainer (Including Hazmat Processes)
- ❯ Machine Operator / Fabricator
- ❯ Consultant
- ❯ Designer
- ❯ Equipment Operator
- ❯ Materials Management

STRATEGY 3
Use Keywords to Match the Vacancy Announcement

Your Outline Format federal resume must include the keywords from the vacancy announcement. Every single USAJOBS announcement contains the important keywords, skills, and keyword phrases that you can copy into your resume for a great match to the announcement.

- ❯ Every USAJOBS announcement has a set of different keywords / phrases.

- ❯ Find keywords in the announcement: Duties, KSAs, Specialized Experience, and the Questionnaire.

- ❯ Keywords will become the ALL CAP HEADLINES.

- ❯ Use at least five to seven keyword phrases for your outline format resume.

Keywords can also come from the Occupational Standards for your job series.
Find them at www.opm.gov/policy-data-oversight/classification-qualifications/classifying-general-schedule-positions/#url=Standards

USAJOBS®
"WORKING FOR AMERICA"

VACANCY ANNOUNCEMENT INFO

JOB TITLE: Emergency Management Specialist, GS-0089-12
DEPARTMENT: Department of the Army
AGENCY U.S. Army Corps of Engineers

DUTIES SECTION (Keywords underlined)

DUTIES:
Serves as senior level <u>Emergency Management</u> Specialist for the South Pacific Division (SPD), <u>Readiness and Contingency</u> Operations Division. Provides <u>technical staff advice</u>, assistance, and planning, coordination, acquisition and maintenance for the Regional Emergency Operations Center (EOC), Emergency Relocation Site, and emergency alternate assemble points. <u>Manages the operational readiness</u> of the Regional Deployable Tactical Operations Center (DTOC), a HQUSACE asset assigned to Sacramento and Los Angeles Districts, and oversees SPD's Planning and Response Team. Ensures operational readiness of the SPD <u>communication systems</u>, <u>emergency information reporting</u> systems and emergency relocation of command and control facilities.

Keywords from Duties:

- EMERGENCY MANAGEMENT
- READINESS AND CONTINGENCY OPERATIONS
- TECHNICAL STAFF ADVICE
- COMMUNICATIONS SYSTEMS AND EMERGENCY INFORMATION REPORTING

Keyword Search **Example Continued**

QUALIFICATIONS SECTION (Keywords underlined)

QUALIFICATIONS REQUIRED:
In order to qualify, you must meet the education and/or experience requirements described below. Your resume must clearly describe your relevant experience; if qualifying based on education, your transcripts will be required as part of your application.

Experience required:
To qualify based on your experience, your resume must describe at least one year of experience which prepared you to do the work in this job. Specialized experience is defined as: Experience <u>engaging Federal, State, local and non-governmental partners</u> which support the <u>development of evacuation plans</u>, strategies, policies and procedures in times of disaster; preparing <u>analysis of data</u>, budgets and contracts; interprets complex <u>policy</u> and <u>prepares reports</u> that outlines complex guidance for the purpose of <u>creating instructions</u>; prepares recommendations, guidance, written and oral summaries for <u>senior level briefings</u>.

Keywords from Specialized Experience:

❯ STATE, LOCAL AND NON-GOVERNMENTAL PARTNERS
❯ EVACUATION PLANS, STRATEGIES
❯ ANALYSIS OF DATA
❯ INTERPRETATION OF COMPLEX POLICY
❯ CREATE INSTRUCTIONS FOR EVACUATIONS

KNOWLEDGE, SKILLS, AND ABILITIES (KSAs) SECTION

You will be evaluated on the basis of your level of competency (knowledge, skills, abilities) in the following areas:
- Knowledge of <u>Emergency Management Operations</u>
- Ability to <u>Develop Emergency Operations Plans</u>
- Ability to <u>Communicate</u>
- Ability to <u>Operate in an Emergency Operations Center</u>

Keywords from the KSAs:

❯ EMERGENCY MANAGEMENT OPERATIONS
❯ DEVELOP EMERGENCY OPERATION PLANS
❯ COMMUNICATIONS
❯ EMERGENCY OPERATIONS CENTER LOGISTICS & OPERATIONS

OUTLINE FORMAT HEADLINES – KEYWORD PHRASES

Primary keywords and headlines and secondary keywords to be described in the paragraph of text.

Work Experience:

Baltimore County Fire Department
1000 Frederick Road
Baltimore, MD   21228 United States

01/2014 - Present
Hours per week: 40
Supervisory Firefighter

Duties, Accomplishments and Related Skills:

EMERGENCY MANAGEMENT OPERATIONS
Emergency Operations Center Logistics and Operations description here

DEVELOP EMERGENCY OPERATION PLANS
Evacuation plans and strategies
Readiness and contingency operations
Create instructions for evaluations

COMMUNICATIONS
State, local and non-governmental partners
Technical staff advice
Communications systems and emergency information reporting

ANALYSIS OF DATA
Interpretation of complex data
Quantitative and qualitative analysis

ACCOMPLISHMENTS
Write a couple of accomplishments that demonstrate the KSAs to stand out and get Best Qualified and Referred

Keyword Search **Example Continued**

USAJOBS SELF-ASSESSMENT QUESTIONNAIRE

Thank you for your interest in an Emergency Management Specialist position with the Department of the Army. **Your resume and the responses you provide to this assessment questionnaire will be used to determine if you are among the best qualified for this position**. Your responses are subject to verification. Please review your responses for accuracy before you submit your application.

Your application will be given a score to determine if you are in the Best Qualified category to be referred to the hiring supervisor for selection.

1. Select the one statement below that best describes the experience that you possess that demonstrates your ability to perform the work of an Emergency Management Specialist at the GS-12 grade level or equivalent pay band in the Federal service.

A. I possess at least one year of specialized experience equivalent to the GS-11 level in the Federal Service which includes experience <u>engaging Federal, State, local and non-governmental partners which support the development of evacuation plans, strategies, policies and procedures in times of disaster; preparing analysis of data, budgets and contracts; interprets complex policy and prepares reports that outlines complex guidance for the purpose of creating instructions; prepares recommendations, guidance, written and oral summaries for senior level briefings associated with emergency situations.</u>
B. I do not possess the experience as described above.

For each task in the following group, choose the statement from the list below that best describes your experience and/or training.
A- I have not had education, training or experience in performing this task.
B- I have had education or training in performing the task, but have not yet performed it on the job.
C- I have performed this task on the job. My work on this task was monitored closely by a supervisor or senior employee to ensure compliance with proper procedures.
D- I have performed this task as a regular part of a job. I have performed it independently and normally without review by a supervisor or senior employee.

E- I am considered an expert in performing this task. I have supervised performance of this task or am normally the person who is consulted by other workers to assist them in doing this task because of my expertise.

Give yourself all the credit you can. You will need to answer E for at least 85% of the questions in order to achieve Best Qualified. If you cannot, then you need not apply.

6. Apply statutory and regulatory requirements (Public Law 84-99, Public Law 93-288 and ER/EP 500-1-1) and mission responsibilities under the Emergency Support Functions to support the <u>National Response Framework and National Disaster Recovery Framework</u>.

7. Perform evaluations, maintenance, revisions and corrective actions of emergency management program plans. Such as <u>preparedness exercises, training, and/or actual emergencies</u> and associated After Action Reviews (AARs) in support of the organizations accreditation.

8. Develop planning documents and procedures pertinent to <u>Deployment and Emergency Operations Center (EOC) operations</u>, Division Continuity of Operations, Catastrophic Disaster and all Hazards.

9. Apply Department of Defense (DoD), US Army Corps of Engineers (USACE), or Federal Emergency Management Agency (FEMA), <u>rules and regulations related to natural disaster and national preparedness</u>, response and recovery to ensure the readiness of the organization.

10. Develop annual <u>budget requirements for emergency management programs and funding sources</u> to stay within budget.

11. Manage regional operations of <u>overseas contingency deployments</u> and Planning and Response team, cadre readiness and deployments.

12. Manage <u>employee data, equipment readiness</u>, disaster event updates, and equipment loan tracking using USACE ENGLink program.

For each response of "E" above, please indicate what position(s) on your resume supports this response (such as title, organization & date). If you fail to include this information, your application will be considered incomplete and you will be removed from consideration for this position.

A. Yes, I verify that all of my responses to this questionnaire are true and accurate. **I accept that if my supporting documentation and/or later steps in the selection process do not support one or more of my responses to the questionnaire that my application may be rated lower and/or I may be removed from further consideration.**

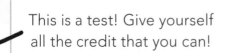

This is a test! Give yourself all the credit that you can!

More Keyword Examples **from Actual Announcements**

LAW ENFORCEMENT SPECIALIST, GS-1800-11

- Technical Operations Specialist
- Plan And Execute Electronic Surveillance
- Expert In Use, Installation And Operation Of Electronic Surveillance Devices
- Investigate Potential Hazards And Implement Electronic Countermeasures
- Conduct Complex Technical Investigations
- Gather Intelligence And Evidence
- Oral And Written Communication
- Perform Lead Technical Security Advances

PROGRAM ANALYST (MOBILIZATION), GS-0343-12

- (Acting) Mobilization Program Specialist
- Program Management
- Personnel Management
- Contract Oversight
- Mobilization Procedures
- Operations Management
- Administrative Planning

PROGRAM ANALYST (WORKFORCE) GS-0343-11

- Director
- Organizational And Workforce Issues Leadership
- Interviews, Surveys, And Focus Groups
- Management, Program, And Data Analysis
- Strategic And Performance Planning/Workforce Development
- Training And Development
- Process Improvement
- Oral And Written Communication
- Data Mining/Trend Analysis
- Workforce Retention Strategy Creation

ADMINISTRATIVE ASSISTANT, GS-0301-7

- Administrative Assistant
- Medical Administrator/Manager
- Demonstrate Knowledge Of Medical Terminology
- Gather Data To Prepare Reports
- Communicate Orally And In Writing

ADMINISTRATIVE OFFICER, GS-0341-9

- Senior Military Advisor/Training
- Training And Program Management
- Management Advisor
- Logistics/Supply Management
- Contract Management
- Communications
- Customer Service
- Served In Liaison Capacity

TECHNICAL WRITER / EDITOR, GS-1082-9

- Technical Writer/Editor
- Research
- Communication .
- Automation
- Workload Management
- Project Research

MARINE TRANSPORTATION SPECIALIST, GS-2150-12

- Marine Transportation Specialist
- Business And Logistics Support
- Project Management
- Analysis
- Quality Assurance
- Emergency Logistics
- Contract Management
- Training
- Knowledge Of Federal, State, And Local Regulations
- Communications And Customer Service

STRATEGY 4 Tell Your Accomplishment Stories

- ❯ Are you proud of a particular project, problem solved, or accomplishment from your last job?

- ❯ How have you made a difference to your organization in the last five years?

- ❯ Supervisors appreciate employees who work hard to meet a mission!

- ❯ Accomplishments are the best way to show how you stand out above the crowd.

Exercise: Start Writing Your Accomplishment Story

What have you accomplished in the last five years that makes you proud, and where you contributed to your organization's mission?

Write several of your key accomplishments here:

_____

_____

_____

_____

_____

_____

_____

_____

_____

Write your story with the Resume Place accomplishment tool
www.resume-place.com/ccar_accomplishment

Key Accomplishment **Examples**

MANAGEMENT AND PROGRAM ANALYST, U.S. NAVY, GS-0343-13
Targeting the same title and grade level

KEY ACCOMPLISHMENTS: Developed and led process and efficiency improvements and cost savings measures that reduced contracts and manpower costs across the enterprise. Provided mission-critical quantitative and qualitative analysis to support decision-making at the highest levels of the Navy, including the initiation of an 8% budget cut. Provided guidance to all regions for more stringent enforcement of entitlement travel expenditures. Cut the $5.4M POM 14 budget to $4.1M. Identified must fund items such as labor and critical contracts for supporting systems Navy Family Accountability System. Replaced personnel support contracts and with military manpower. Developed a POM Capability Plan. Re-evaluated baseline program requirements for POM 14.

DIRECTOR OF NAVY-MARINE CORPS RELIEF SOCIETY
Targeting: Program Analyst, Government Agency, GS 12

KEY ACCOMPLISHMENTS: Streamlined the staff onboarding process, resulting in an increase of over 85 new staff members stationed in four (4) offices throughout the region. Promoted three (3) times in three (3) years to become the first female and first civilian in the history of the organization to lead the Camp Pendleton offices. Revolutionized the workforce training and development for the region by launching the organization's first annual training week. Selected to serve as one of the organization's primary field media liaisons for the Wall Street Journal, ABC News, and others.

OWNER / OPERATOR / GENERAL CONTRACTOR
Targeting Maintenance Supervisor, Smithsonian, WS-4701-10

KEY ACCOMPLISHMENTS: Converted 1,000 sf of a 1920 original historical Carriage House into commercial office space. Effecitvely managed project with $70 budget, including build-out of office space: metal stud drywall framing, electrical sub-panel, lights, plugs, switches, drywall finishes, floor finishes, split HVAC system. Supervised an 8-person crew.

BILINGUAL CUSTOMER SERVICE REPRESENTATIVE
Targeting Bilingual Contact Representative, SSA , GS-0962-6

KEY ACCOMPLISHMENTS: Initiated policy of encouraging customers to use in-store self-service kiosk. The largely Spanish-speaking clientele were hesitant to use the kiosk with its English prompts and instead elected to stand in line, exacerbating wait times for all in-store customers. I would identify a hesitant user and approach him/her in a friendly manner, walking the customer through the steps needed to pay a bill or perform another simple task at the kiosk. Other staff members followed suit, and it is now standard policy. Wait times have also decreased overall due to the number of customers now using the self-service kiosk.

Lead Transportation Security Inspector-Aviation, SV-1801-I
Targeting Lead Transportation Security Officer, SV-1802-J

KEY ACCOMPLISHMENTS: During a championship tournament, which brought a large number of visitors and high-profile VIPs to the local county airport, I liaised with tournament planner concerning schedule in order to plan and alert screeners of heavy flight activities and equipment being carried on board. Resolved a major significant golf bag problem that required hand carrying, due to late flight for a significant tournament deadline. Recognized for outstanding customer services by top golf pro in the country.

Using the CCAR Format

The Office of Personnel Management has a recommended format for writing KSAs and your accomplishments record in a story-telling format: the Context, Challenge, Action, Result (CCAR) Model for writing better KSAs. This CCAR story-telling format is also great for the Behavior-Based Interview.

CONTEXT

The context should include the role you played in this example. Were you a team member, planner, organizer, facilitator, administrator, or coordinator? Also, include your job title at the time and the timeline of the project. You may want to note the name of the project or situation.

CHALLENGE

What was the specific problem that you faced that needed resolution? Describe the challenge of the situation. The problem could be disorganization in the office, new programs that needed to be implemented or supported, a change in management, a major project stalled, or a large conference or meeting being planned. The challenge can be difficult to write about. You can write the challenge last when you are drafting your KSAs.

ACTION

What did you do that made a difference? Did you change the way the office processed information, responded to customers, managed programs? What did you do?

RESULT

What difference did it make? Did this new action save dollars or time? Did it increase accountability and information? Did the team achieve its goals?

Write your story with the Resume Place accomplishment tool
www.resume-place.com/ccar_accomplishment

Ten Tips for **Writing Great Accomplishment Stories**

1

One excellent example per narrative will demonstrate that you have the knowledge, skills, and abilities for the position.

2

If possible and appropriate, use a different example in each accomplishment statement.

3

The typical length is 300 words or less.

4

Write your accomplishment examples with specific details, including the challenge of the example and the results.

5

Spell out ALL acronyms.

6

Write in the first person: "I serve as a point-of-contact for all inquiries that come to our office."

7

Quantify your results and accomplishments.

8

Draw material from all parts of your life, including community service, volunteer projects, or training.

9

Limit your paragraphs to 6 to 8 lines long for readability.

10

Proofread your writing again and again.

Practice Writing the **CCAR Format**

Select two of your accomplishments and record the Context, Challenge, Action, Result (CCAR) of those accomplishments.

Context

Challenge

Action

Result

Write your accomplishments in the CCAR format with this free Resume Place tool:
www.resume-place.com/ccar_accomplishment

Context

Challenge

Action

Result

STRATEGY 5
Add Your Core Competencies

Texas Military Forces - LONE STAR VALUES

Loyalty	Bear true faith and allegiance to the State & Nation, Mission & Family
Opportunity	Cultivate an environment for ALL to excel
Networked	Connect to communities, families, interagency partners and components
Ethics	Honor the public trust, exceed standards and expectations
Selfless Service	Place the welfare of the Texas Military Forces, State and Nation first
Texas Spirit	Embrace the courageous spirit of our people, history and culture
Adaptability	Act with understanding, innovation, resourcefulness, flexibility & urgency
Ready	Prepare mentally, physically and spiritually to deploy at home and abroad

Besides specialized experience, education, and technical skills, what "value-added" competencies can you offer a supervisor?

What Are Competencies?

OPM defines a competency as a measurable pattern of knowledge, skills, abilities, behaviors, and other characteristics that an individual needs to perform work roles or occupational functions successfully. "Competencies can be seen as *basic qualities that employees should exhibit in the work place to maximize their potential for the government.*"

Core Competencies Are Your Transferable Skills!

If you are changing your career, these core competencies will demonstrate that you have valuable skills that are transferable to your new career.

How Do I Use Core Competencies When Applying for Jobs?

These characteristics go above and beyond skills. You can stand out in a government resume, question/essay narrative, or behavior-based interview by highlighting these competencies. Determine the top five or ten competencies that make you a stand-out employee in your field of work. Add these competencies to your resume in the work experience descriptions for a stronger federal resume!

Office of Personnel Management (OPM) **Core Competencies**

Find your core competencies and check them off the list. Add a few of these competencies into the "duties" section of your work experience.

Interpersonal Effectiveness

❑ Builds and sustains positive relationships.

❑ Handles conflicts and negotiations effectively.

❑ Builds and sustains trust and respect.

❑ Collaborates and works well with others.

❑ Shows sensitivity and compassion for others.

❑ Encourages shared decision-making.

❑ Recognizes and uses ideas of others.

❑ Communicates clearly, both orally and in writing.

❑ Listens actively to others.

❑ Honors commitments and promises.

Customer Service

❑ Understands that customer service is essential to achieving our mission.

❑ Understands and meets the needs of internal customers.

❑ Manages customer complaints and concerns effectively and promptly.

❑ Designs work processes and systems that are responsive to customers.

❑ Ensures that daily work and the strategic direction are customer-centered.

❑ Uses customer feedback data in planning and providing products and services.

❑ Encourages and empowers subordinates to meet or exceed customer needs and expectations.

❑ Identifies and rewards behaviors that enhance customer satisfaction.

Flexibility/Adaptability

❑ Responds appropriately to new or changing situations.

❑ Handles multiple inputs and tasks simultaneously.

❑ Seeks and welcomes the ideas of others.

❑ Works well with all levels and types of people.

❑ Accommodates new situations and realities.

❑ Remains calm in high-pressure situations.

❑ Makes the most of limited resources.

❑ Demonstrates resilience in the face of setbacks.

❑ Understands change management.

Creative Thinking

- ☐ Appreciates new ideas and approaches.
- ☐ Thinks and acts innovatively.
- ☐ Looks beyond current reality and the "status quo".
- ☐ Demonstrates willingness to take risks.
- ☐ Challenges assumptions.
- ☐ Solves problems creatively.
- ☐ Demonstrates resourcefulness.
- ☐ Fosters creative thinking in others.
- ☐ Allows and encourages employees to take risks.
- ☐ Identifies opportunities for new projects and acts on them.
- ☐ Rewards risk-taking and non-successes and values what was learned.

Systems Thinking

- ☐ Understands the complexities of the agency and how the "product" is delivered.
- ☐ Appreciates the consequences of specific actions on other parts of the system.
- ☐ Thinks in context.
- ☐ Knows how one's role relates to others in the organization.
- ☐ Demonstrates awareness of the purpose, process, procedures, and outcomes of one's work.
- ☐ Encourages and rewards collaboration.

Organizational Stewardship

- ☐ Demonstrates commitment to people.
- ☐ Empowers and trusts others.
- ☐ Develops leadership skills and opportunities throughout organization.
- ☐ Develops team-based improvement processes.
- ☐ Promotes future-oriented system change.
- ☐ Supports and encourages lifelong learning throughout the organization.
- ☐ Manages physical, fiscal, and human resources to increase the value of products and services.
- ☐ Builds links between individuals and groups in the organization.
- ☐ Integrates organization into the community.
- ☐ Accepts accountability for self, others, and the organization's development.
- ☐ Works to accomplish the organizational business plan.

Core Competencies Blended into the Outline Format

John is a former Sous Chef who was hired as Program Analyst with FEMA as GS-12. Now he is a GS-14 working in Disaster Preparedness.

SOUS CHEF
Government House, State of Maryland
110 State Circle Annapolis, MD 21401
Supervisor: Susan B. Arnold, 410-333-4444, May be contacted.

06/20xx to Present [8 years]
Salary: $60,000 per year
40 hours/week

Serve as second in command of kitchen staff for First Family of Maryland. Manage kitchen operations and direct staff to ensure efficient business processes and customer satisfaction.

Operations Management: Direct daily operations of full-service kitchen, planning, coordinating, and preparing formal and informal meals and events for up to 3,000 people, both planned in advance and last minute, with range of guests from international dignitaries to constituents. Continually analyze operations, procedures, and policies to achieve highest efficiency and best practices. Recommend and implement range of process improvement initiatives. Implement, apply, and interpret policies, regulations, and directives. Work with senior management to establish goals and objectives.

Project Management, Analysis and Workflow Management: Conduct needs assessment surveys and determine needs based on event specifications and labor demands. Plan event with consideration to protocol, preferences, caliber of event, attendees, and lead time. Create project timeline and assign, monitor, and adjust tasks according to staff strengths/weaknesses to fulfill deadline completion. Review progress and make production and priority adjustments as needed. Manage multiple task lists to complete projects with adjacent deadlines. Resolve problems and issues, including crisis situations. Conduct post-event assessment to identify successes and areas for improvement. (Creativity and resourcefulness, problem-solving)

Supply Management: Take inventory and plan orders to regulate flow of product and ensure stock levels meet event and daily needs. Research best products and vendors to comply with state purchasing regulations; establish delivery protocols and resolve delivery problems. Rotate stock, monitor usage and storage to ensure efficiency, sanitation, and security, and reduce waste. Negotiate, administer, and oversee vendor and service contracts. Maintain documentation, verify invoices, and assure prompt payment.

Budgeting / Funds Management: Develop pricing and cost accounting procedures. Analyze and forecast product and labor costs estimates. Apply due diligence to projects to ensure feasibility and cost effectiveness, as well as conduct after-action reviews. Compile budget information and apply generally accepted accounting procedures and state regulations to track expenditures, including petty cash. Perform cost and price and comparative analyses. Develop and implement pricing and marketing information for clients. Identify and resolve budget issues and develop cost-cutting solutions to ensure budget adherence. Brief management and recommend cost control improvements and budget adjustments. (Systems Thinking, Problem-solving)

Logistics Management: Integrate logistics of event planning, including manpower and personnel, supply, training, storage, and facilities. Research and plan manpower, equipment, and fiscal resources.

Personnel Management: Direct kitchen and wait staff, promoting teamwork and communication. Provide continual training and coaching to improve employee performance, job knowledge, and career advancement; also, serve as point of contact for benefit information. Write position descriptions and assist in hiring process. Resolve employee issues and provide employee input and feedback to management. Assist in background checks for auxiliary employees and vendors. Train others in security and privacy protection. (Team Leader, Interpersonal Skills)

Customer Service: Serve as personal and administrative assistant to First Family. Anticipate and respond to needs, maintaining flexible and service-oriented attitude. Purchase personal and business related goods, including supplies, as extension of house staff. Assist in managing schedule and making travel arrangements and appointment reservations, as needed. Protect privacy of First Family and work with Maryland State Police to ensure security precautions are followed at all times. (Customer Services)

Communications: Build rapport with internal staff and external departments to improve operations and flow of information. Respond to written and verbal inquires from the public and the media, adhering to strict communication standards. Represent First Family at charity and press events. (Communications)

Information Management: Develop and utilize spreadsheets, databases, and professional documents to improve operational readiness, manage projects, and research information. Maintain records on events, including menus, demographics, and after-action reports. Assist in establishing database for mailing list.

Key Accomplishments:
- Plan, coordinate, and execute breakfast, lunch, dinner for First Family and other events, including seated dinners and open houses for up to 4,000, with usually 3-5 events per week, as many as 2 per day. (Efficiency and effectiveness)
- Instituted process changes to increase efficiency and change mind-set from reactive to proactive. Created plan to work one meal ahead, allowing time to respond to last minute requests, changes, and events. (Efficiency and Effectiveness)
- Received letter of appreciation from the White House for organizing luncheon attended by President Bill Clinton with less than 24-hour notice. (Customer Services)
- Implemented industrial production system, automated systems and information management for production, scheduling, and cost control. (Resourceful)
- Actively built team mindset and morale and implemented employee incentive program, stressing interdepartmental cooperation and employees' role in organizational success.
- Resulted in improved attendance and performance. (Team Lead, Mentor)

STRATEGY 6

Edit Carefully

_!_

The Office of Personnel Management recommends PLAIN LANGUAGE _for your resume._

Words to **Avoid:**

- ❯ Responsible for / Responsibilities include
- ❯ Duties include
- ❯ Other / Additional Duties include
- ❯ Helped with / in
- ❯ Worked with / in
- ❯ Assisted with
- ❯ Participate in
- ❯ Perform (overused in government resumes)
- ❯ Prepare (overused in government resumes)
- ❯ Serve as
- ❯ Involved in / with

Visit www.opm.gov/information-management/plain-language/

At the heart of every good sentence is a strong, precise verb. The converse is true as well—at the core of most confusing, awkward, or wordy sentences lies a weak verb. Try to use the active voice whenever possible.

Can you find the Passive Voice Phrases?
Underline the words that should be edited out of this resume:

PASSIVE VOICE—Duties:

Serve as a staff action officer in the Engineering and Implementation Division. Responsible for overseeing the establishment of new information systems and capabilities. Managing the modernization of existing facilities for the European Theater. Other duties include coordinating and integrating technical aspects of communications and automation working with administrative and management matters. Help in evaluating overall requirements. Made recommendation in policy. Involved with justifying funding equipment requirements, procurement and support services. Utilized my expertise in the overall concepts, theories, analytical processes and techniques of communications/automation, for the requirements of the command. I coordinated and lead assigned projects and reported, directed command project development. Provided advice and assistance on probable impact of proposed standardized systems, new equipment configurations. ADP equipment interface. Work in a lab environment to help support in any Technical assistance as the third tier.

ACTIVE VOICE—Duties:

STAFF ACTION OFFICER in the Engineering and Implementation Division. Oversee the establishment of new information systems and capabilities. Manage the modernization of existing facilities for the European Theater. Coordinate and integrate technical aspects of communications and automation working with administrative and management matters. Evaluate overall requirements.

RECOMMEND POLICY AND JUSTIFY FUNDING equipment requirements, procurement and support services. Utilize my expertise in the overall concepts, theories, analytical processes and techniques of communications/automation, for the requirements of the command. Coordinate and lead assigned projects and reported, directed command project development.

ADVISOR AND THIRD TIER TECHNICAL ASSISTANCE on probable impact of proposed standardized systems, new equipment configurations in a lab environment to help support ADP interface.

Use Powerful Words

This list of more than 100 powerful words for resume writing is pulled together based on many years of professional resume writing experience. There are undoubtedly many more, but this set should get you started.

Creation
assemble
conceive
convene
create
design
forge
form
formulate
invent
implement
initiate
realize
spearhead
plan

Employment
deploy
employ
exercise
use
utilize

Quality
excellent
great
good
high quality
outstanding
quality
special
superb

Success
accomplish
achieve
attain
master
score (a victory)
succeed
sustain

Primacy
advisor
coworker
key
major
expert
primary
principal
subject matter
source person
lead
sole source

Authorship
author
create
draft
edit
generate
publish
write

Leadership
administer
control
direct
govern
head up
lead
manage
oversee
run
supervise

Outcomes
communication
cooperation
cost-effective
efficiency
morale
outcomes
output
productivity

Persuasion
coach
galvanize
inspire
lobby
rally
persuade
(re)invigorate
(re)vitalize
unify
unite

Competencies
able
adept at
capable
competent
demonstrated
effective
expert
knowledgeable
proven
skilled
tested
trained
versed in

Degree
completely
considerably
effectively
fully
especially
extremely
outstanding
greatly
particularly
powerful
seasoned
highly
significantly
strongly
thoroughly
solidly

Newness
creative
first-ever
first-of-its-kind
innovative
novel
state-of-the-art

First or Only
chief
first
foremost
greatest
most
leading
number-one
singular
one
only
prime
single
sole
unparalleled
top
unique
unrivaled

Here are a few before and after examples of better word choices for your resume.

Currently I am working as the Manager of Operations.
> Manage operations.

I have experience with planning meetings.
> Plan and coordinate meetings.

I have helped set up office systems.
> Organized new office systems.

Major duties include working with other staff.
> Cooperated with staff.

I used a variety of equipment.
> Equipment skills include...

Worked in the capacity of management analyst
> Management Analyst

I was responsible for managing the daily operations.
> Managed daily operations.

When needed, supervise team members.
> Supervise team members on occasion.

Being the timekeeper for the office
> Timekeeper for the office

Assisted with planning, researching, and designing...
> Planned, researched, and designed...

My other duties consist of customer services, research, and problem-solving.
> Research and resolve problems for customers.

Assisted in all aspects of...
> Involved in all aspects of...

The information is gathered from...
> Compiled, organized, and managed information gathered from...

Worked with team members
> Member of a team

Beware of **Acronyms**

We know that federal employees depend on acronyms to communicate, but acronyms could make your resume sound like Greek to an HR specialist or hiring manager who is not familiar with your exact line of work.

Make sure you spell out your acronyms and give a definition if needed. For example. WAWF (Wide Area Work Flow) could be described this way in your resume:

> Train and provide technical assistance to customers in the use of Wide Area Work Flow (WAWF), the Department of Defense Receipts & Acceptance system.

Be Constent with **Verb Tenses**

The rule about tense in resumes is to use present tense for all present responsibilities and skills and past tense for all past responsibilities. For example:

SENIOR COMPUTER TECHNICIAN (September 20XX to present)

- Senior Computer Technician serving a fast-paced metropolitan retail outlet for Best Buy, one of the nation's leading retailers and resellers of technology products and services. Lead for the Technical Service Group, a 7-person team providing warranty repair services for the broad range of computer and personal electronics products sold by the company. Repair desktop and laptop computer systems, including digital camera equipment, smartphones, printers, and other computer peripherals.

SENIOR COMPUTER TECHNICIAN (September 20XX to June 20XX)

- Systems administrator for a scientific workgroup computing environment. Planned and delivered customer support services to the organization. Installed, upgraded, delivered, and provided troubleshooting for hardware and software components. Performed file back-ups and restores, system and peripherals troubleshooting, and component repair.

- Provided a high level of customer service for a wide variety of computer and network problems. Monitored, analyzed, and resolved end-user issues and provided informal training and assistance.

- Researched and reported on new technologies, equipment, and software with application to the Naval Surface Warfare Center.

In the old days, there was no "I" in a resume. This was probably because it is easy to fall into the trap of starting every sentence with "I," which quickly becomes tedious and egocentric-sounding. The downside to avoiding "I" is that the sentences can end up as verbal contortionism. Today, the resume writer must strike a balance between these extremes. The modern rule of thumb is to use "I" to personalize your resume, but not so often as to become obnoxious.

"I Rules"

❯ **Don't** use "I" to start every sentence.

❯ **Don't** use "I" twice in the same sentence, or in two sentences in a row.

❯ **Do** use "I" when it makes your sentence flow smoothly.

❯ **Do** use "I" three to five times per page.

❯ **Do** use "I" with descriptions of accomplishments or "KSAs in the resume."

❯ **Do** use "I" in a compelling sentence emphasizing complexity, uniqueness, challenge, or outstanding service.

❯ **Do** use "I" in a summary of skills or competencies.

❯ **Do** use "I" in project descriptions where you are performing a particular role.

❯ **Do** use "I" in your Other Qualifications or Summary of Skills section. You can use "I" more frequently in a summary of your personal values, core competencies, and skills.

Here are two examples of good form when using "I":

My Division Director ordered an audit to be conducted within two business days. The task appeared nearly impossible. After getting input from other team members, I proposed a division of labor that made the challenge more manageable. We completed the audit a half-day ahead of schedule, and the Director awarded me a Certificate of Recognition for my contribution.

After extensive research I was able to convey to all personnel covering 7 different agencies the proper use/dispatch of government vehicles within Europe. Status of Forces Agreement (SOFA) stipulates if a European country is not part of this agreement, government vehicles cannot be driven there without proper authorization.

STRATEGY 7

Submit Your Resume in USAJOBS Correctly

USAJOBS Navigation Quick Tips

- The most frequent way to apply for a competitive federal job online is on USAJOBS.gov.

- Follow the directions!

- Use the USAJOBS builder instead of the resume upload feature to avoid omission of required information, or pay careful attention to the required information when creating your upload resume.

- Make sure to submit required documents.

- 11:59 pm Eastern Time (ET) is the typical deadline.

My Account Main Page

- Profile: Personal Information, Hiring Eligibility, Preferences, Demographic Information, and Account Information

- Resumes: You can save up to five resumes in USAJOBS. That includes uploaded resumes and resumes built using the USAJOBS Resume Builder.

- Saved Searches: Save your preferences for jobs you've searched in the past.

- Saved Jobs: You can bookmark jobs you like.

- Saved Documents: Your uploaded documents appear here. If you are using education to qualify for experience, you must upload your transcripts. They can be unofficial (HR will ask for official transcripts if you are hired).

- Application Status: This section helps you track and follow up on your application and determine if you've actually applied.

Getting Started on **USAJOBS**

Logging In: Write Down Your Password!

Applicants routinely complain that they forget their password, which must include numbers, symbols, and letters. Make sure you link your account to a personal email, not a work email, so that you can access it at home.

Edit Your Profile: Answer Carefully!

The profile section of USAJOBS will pop up when you register or can be accessed by clicking on "Edit Profile" on the Main page. You will be asked to enter Contact Information, Hiring Eligibility, Preferences, Demographic Information, and Account Information.

Your SSN will not be required in USAJOBS. But you might have to add your SSN and DOB into the questionnaire application system.

My Account

Profile

Resumes

Saved Searches

Inbox (3)

Saved Jobs

Saved Documents

Application Status

☑Contact Information ☑Hiring Eligibility ☑Other ☑Demographic ☑Account Information

Please Note: Fields with an (*) are **required fields.**

Legal Name ❓

Prefix	First Name *	Middle Name	Last Name *	Suffix
--Select--	KATHRYN	K	TROUTMAN	--Select--

Address ❓

Address 1 *   655 West Lake Road

Address 2

Country *   United States

Postal Code *   City/Town *   State/Territory/Province *

21228   Catonsville   Maryland

Telephone ❓

Telephone 1 *   Day Phone   907-333-3333   Ext:

Telephone 2   --Select--   Ext:

Telephone 3   --Select--   Ext:

Email

Primary Email Address *   kathryn@resume-place.com

Secondary Email Address

What is my Secondary Email Address used for?

What is your email format preference? ❓ ◉ HTML ◯ Text
Some email providers block HTML messages. Select "Text" to ensure your emails go through.

Be advised that only one account can be created for each email address. Be sure the email account you use is only accessible by you and the email account is properly secured.

Cancel   **Save**   **Next**

Contact Information

Be sure to enter an email address for your home, not work. In the event that you forget your password, the system may need to contact you via email for confirmation. You want to make sure you have listed an email address that you can always access.

Email

Primary Email Address * `kathryn@resume-place.com`

Secondary Email Address [   ]
What is my Secondary Email Address used for?

What is your email format preference? ❓ ◉ HTML ○ Text
Some email providers block HTML messages. Select "Text" to ensure your emails go through.

Be advised that only one account can be created for each email address. Be sure the email account you use is only accessible by you and the email account is properly secured.

Eligibility

Your answers to these questions can determine whether or not your resume and application ever make it to Human Resources. So, answer carefully.

U.S. Citizen: Most federal jobs require citizenship.

Selective Service: If you are a man, did you sign up for the draft? Many times you may not remember doing so, but it is a normal part of getting a driver's license, voting, etc.

Contractors do not have "reinstatement eligibility."

Current and Former Federal Employees: Select the appropriate answer regarding federal employment status and reinstatement eligibility. Also answer questions about your agency, organization, pay plan, series, and grade level/pay.

---

4. Please select the statement below which best reflects your federal employment status (if applicable). * ❓

   ○ I am not and have never been a federal civilian employee.

   ◉ I am currently a federal civilian employee.

   ○ I am a former federal civilian employee with reinstatement eligibility.

   ○ I am a former federal civilian employee but do not have reinstatement eligibility.

Getting Started on USAJOBS

- By which Federal agency and organization are you currently employed?

Select Department: `Department Of Homeland Security ▲▼`

Select Agency: `Transportation Security Administration ▲▼`

- Indicate the pay plan, series, grade level/pay band of the highest permanent graded position you ever held as a Federal Civilian Employee. (Question does not apply to members of the armed forces covered under Title 10.)

Pay Plan: `GS – General Schedule ▲▼`

Occupational Series: `0342 Support Services Administration ▲▼`

Highest Pay Grade: `09`

Eligibility Documentation

Veterans

When claiming preference, veterans must provide a copy of their DD-214, Certificate of Release or Discharge from Active Duty, or other acceptable documentation.

Applicants claiming 10 point preference will need to submit Form SF-15, "Application for 10-Point Veteran Preference". Ensure your documentation reflects the character of discharge.

If you do not upload your documentation, you will not be eligible for veterans' preference.

Federal Employees

If you are a current federal employee, you must upload your SF-50, or you will not be considered for jobs open only to current feds.

Sometimes they will ask for your last year's evaluation. Make sure it is signed.

Veterans' Document Upload:

When claiming veterans' preference, preference eligibles must provide a copy of their DD 214, Certificate of Release or Discharge from Active Duty, or other acceptable documentation. Applicants claiming 10 point preference will need to submit an SF-15, Application for 10-point Veterans' Preference.

For current service members who have not yet been discharged, a certification letter of expected discharge or release from active duty within 120 days under honorable conditions is required at the time of application. Ensure your documentation reflects the character of discharge.

Document Title: `_____`

Document Type: ❓ Select Document:
`DD-214 ▲▼` `Choose File` No file chosen

Files must be less than 3mb and can be in one of the following formats: GIF, JPG, JPEG, PNG, RTF, PDF, or Word (DOC or DOCX).

`Upload`   `Cancel`

Other - Important Questions!

Applicants should choose carefully in this section because their answers will determine whether they are eligible later.

Are you willing to travel? If you say "No" you will be disqualified from a job, even if the amount of travel is very minimal. Be sure that you can travel at least 25% in case you must attend a conference.

What type of work are you willing to accept? Consider that more federal agencies are using "temp" and "term" jobs to fill positions when money is tight, or when the future is unknown. For example, many jobs that came out of the mortgage crisis were initially term jobs that eventually may become permanent.

If you accidentally apply for a "temp" or "term" job, but didn't click the button on this page, your application won't be read at all by Human Resources.

What type of work schedule are you willing to accept? Consider being flexible.

Select your desired work location(s). Select all of U.S. and if you apply for a job abroad, remember to come back and select that location as well.

If you only pick D.C., you might later be disqualified for a job in the Maryland or Virginia D.C. suburbs.

Demographic

Your answers to this question are voluntary and do not affect whether or not you will be hired.

Personal Information

Write down your password! Also, you can choose to receive "Notification Alerts" on your application. This is important in case a job posting is pulled or re-announced.

Notification Settings

Notification Alerts enable you to stay informed of changes to your application status.

Select the items that you would like to be notified of via your primary email. You may edit your preferences and unsubscribe at any time.

- ☑ When jobs I have started an application for have closed.
- ☑ When jobs I have saved are scheduled to close in three calendar days.
- ☑ When the status of an application I've submitted changes.

Cancel   Previous   Save   Finish

USAJOBS Resume Builder vs. Upload

Once you have set up your USAJOBS account and profile, it's time to add your resumes. either by manually entering your resume in the resume builder or uploading a complete resume from your computer.

Using the USAJOBS Resume Builder increases the chances that you will apply correctly for a federal job by making sure you complete all required fields. If you upload a federal resume into USAJOBS, make sure you include all of the details that are marked as "required" in the USAJOBS Resume Builder, such as the month and year for employment start and end dates.

An uploaded resume, on the other hand, allows you to be more creative with the organization and the format of your resume, such as adding a profile or skills summary at the top of the resume, putting the education section first if you are a student or recent grad, or designing an eye-catching resume (but keep it conservative for the federal workplace).

Store up to five resumes in USAJOBS.

Resume 1: MSW Veterans Administrati...
View | Edit | Duplicate | Delete

Status: Not Searchable
Make Searchable

Format: USAJOBS Resume
Source: Built with USAJOBS Resume Builder

Resume 2: IT Spec, Customer Service...
View | Edit | Duplicate | Delete

Status: Not Searchable
Make Searchable

Format: USAJOBS Resume
Source: Built with USAJOBS Resume Builder

Resume 3: IT Specialist Veteran JS ...
View | Edit | Duplicate | Delete

Status: Not Searchable
Make Searchable

Format: USAJOBS Resume
Source: Built with USAJOBS Resume Builder

Resume 4: Air Traffic Controller (T...
View | Edit | Duplicate | Delete

Status: Not Searchable
Make Searchable

Format: USAJOBS Resume
Source: Built with USAJOBS Resume Builder

> Build New Resume   Upload New Resume

You have created **4** of **5** possible resumes. You are able to upload and store **5** resumes to your My USAJOBS account.

Use the Resume Builder to create your resume from start to finish

Create a resume in a word processing file and upload into USAJOBS

Resume - Select one of your stored USAJOBS resumes to send :
○ MSW Veterans Administration
○ IT Spec, Customer Service, GS-2210-11
○ IT Specialist Veteran JS Guide 5th
○ Air Traffic Controller (Trainee)
○ Resume for CDP

Attachment(s) - Select one or more of your Saved Documents to send (or first Save Job and Upload Documents). :
☐ COVER (Class Notes Fedres Writing)
☐ COVER (ED Cover Letter)

Fields below with an asterisks (*) are required.

* ☐ I have previewed my resume . The selected document includes the information I wish to provide with this application.

☐ Allow me to attach demographic information to the application. Review or update your demographic information.

* ☐ I certify, to the best of my knowledge and belief, all the information submitted by me with my application for employment is true, complete, and made in good faith, and that I have truthfully and accurately represented my work experience, knowledge, skills, abilities and education (degrees, accomplishments, etc.). I understand that the information provided may be investigated. I understand that misrepresenting my experience or education, or providing false or fraudulent information in or with my application may be grounds for not hiring me or for firing me after I begin work. I also understand that false or fraudulent statements may be punishable by fine or imprisonment (18 U.S.C. 1001).

| Apply for this position now! | Cancel |

When you apply for a position on USAJOBS, you will need to choose which resume in your account you will use to apply.

Be sure to choose the correct resume!

If the agency is using Application Manager as the Automated Recruitment System for their questionnaire and document collection, you will be taken to this site automatically from USAJOBS.

Complete the Self-Assessment Questions and upload the required documents.

Ready to Submit?

Submit My Answers

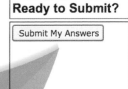

IMPORTANT! Be sure to follow the step through the entire application process and to click "SUBMIT MY ANSWERS."

You MUST click this button in order for your application to be submitted.

Sample USAJOBS Builder Resume

Mark Glenville
2220 Alexandria Drive
Alexandria, VA 22408 US
Mobile: 555-555-5555
Email: mglenville@gmail.com

Availability: **Job Type:** Permanent, Temporary, Term, Telework
Work Schedule: Full-Time

Desired locations: United States
Germany
France

Work Experience: **General Service Administration**
Government Travel Charge Card Team
4800 Mark Center Drive, Suite 04J25-01
Alexandria , VA   22350-9000 United States

07/2014 - Present
Salary: 99,905.00 USD Per Year
Hours per week: 40
Series: 0343 **Pay Plan:** GS **Grade:** 13
Program Analyst, GS -0343-13 (This is a federal job)
Duties, Accomplishments and Related Skills:

FINANCIAL OVERSIGHT: Resolve issues and concerns and monitor monthly reporting results such as mission critical status and salary offset enrollment. Confirm that Component Program Managers (CPM's) monitor and addressing the status of accounts to ensure compliance with key financial metrics. Monitor reports to identify potential fraud, waste, and abuse, elevating concerns for information and resolution. Submit monthly reports with analysis of concerns.

TRAINING IN CREDIT CARD PROCEDURES: Liaison for tenant agencies on the Government Travel Charge Card Team (GTCC). GSA manages one of largest Travel Card Program in the world with yearly volume in excess of $1 billion. Work with the CPMs to identify and resolve any problems, issues, and requested enhancements related to the electronic access system (EAS). Coordinate with Suntrust Bank and the GTCC team training point of contact to assist with ad-hoc training requests as well as concerns raised by CPMs regarding perceived training deficiencies. Offer training assistance, such as providing information and answering questions on the GSA SmartPay Forum, National Capital Region training at Bank Facility in Richmond, VA.

CUSTOMER SERVICES AND PROBLEM-SOLVING: Provide excellent and responsive customer service to senior Air Force and Agency

This resume is an excerpt of a resume created in the USAJOBS builder to show you what a resume looks like when printed from USAJOBS.

executives. Ensure issues and concerns are addressed and resolved or surfaced to the appropriate leadership and follow up through resolution. Coordinate customer needs with Suntrust.

BUSINESS DEVELOPMENT: Participate in senior level meetings with CPM staff, Suntrust and other program stakeholders. Attend quarterly reviews and submit written report on critical points of interest. Conduct program management and oversight to verify compliance.

MONITOR BUSINESS PROCESSES: Compile potential changes and coordinate draft document with the CPMs and DTMO leadership. Re-write and transition to GSA Instruction format. Monitor program compliance and all related policies with the OMB Circular A-123, Appendix B requirements. Report cases of non-compliance and recommended DoD policy resolutions.

ANALYZE AGENCY GOALS AND PERFORMANCE MEASURES: Use IntelliLink, one of our best analytics tools provided by Visa Corp for charge card statistics and CCRS and CCMS, two other analytics systems provided by Suntrust to pull reports and monitor individual accounts. Promote data initiatives, such as communications efforts, audits, chip, and PIN implementation. Provide analysis and assistance as required. Research and coordinate through Citi EAS, IntelliLink, or other applicable sources.

KEY ACCOMPLISHMENTS:

-Received Above and Beyond award for expertise on Visa payment Security and Technology in the DTMO. Briefed the Director on Visa Forum after attending in May 2015. Director was so impressed that he wanted me to provide the same brief to executive Director. Briefed directors on the U.S. chip migration, the benefits of the chip, and how chip technology works. Presented a digital payments update and shared Advancing Consumer Authentication, including managing fraud through analytics. The DHRA Director requested me to provide the same briefing to entire DTMO organization.

-Led successful pilot of Chip and PIN cards and expansion of issuance/use to the larger GSA population (1.6M cardholders). Led organization communications for this effort. Developed extensive communication and training material with key messaging for both program administrators and cardholders. Also led Audit response by drafting 'sound-bites' and a response to the draft audit. Resulted in completion of work by established deadlines.
Supervisor: Sam Smith (703-333-3333)
Okay to contact this Supervisor: Yes

Sample USAJOBS Builder Resume

Dawson Christopher
388 East-West Highway
Orlando, FL 32466 US
Mobile: 2022020022 - Ext:
Day Phone: 8502020022 - Ext:
Email: christopher.dawson@live.com

Availability:

Job Type: Permanent, Temporary, Term, Detail, Seasonal, Summer, Presidential Management Fellows, Recent Graduates, Multiple Appointment Types, Intermittent, Internships, Telework
Work Schedule: Full-Time, Part-Time, Shift Work, Intermittent, Job Sharing

---

Work Experience:

Target
2345 Highway 22
Panama City, FL 32405 United States

08/20xx - Present
Salary: 10.04 USD Per Hour
Hours per week: 30
Backroom Associate
Duties, Accomplishments and Related Skills:
USE OF COMPUTER SOFTWARE TO STORE INFORMATION: Maintain Target Enterprise Database to track inventory and update database promptly and accurately when new stock arrives. Create daily inventory reports to verify drastic count report and backroom report for accurate inventory management. Review data to identify general sales trends.

DATA TRACKING AND REPORTING: Supervise team of inventory control specialists who collect inventory data. Compile data into reports, identify general sales trends, and present sales information to senior store management. Review inventory reports and document loss or theft through Count Adjustment Store form via Target intranet. Communicate inventory loss or theft with the management team and the Asset Prevention team.

MERCHANDISE AND STOCK MANAGEMENT: Organize merchandise throughout a large retail store to maintain shelves' appearance and product availability. Comply with corporate policies, procedures and regulatory requirements. Prepare sales and inventory reports for corporate office.

PHYSICAL AND AUTOMATED INVENTORY MANAGEMENT: Take inventory; track inventory discrepancies; examine merchandise to identify and document items to be reordered or replenished. Drive profitable sale through the use of inventory management tools.

TEAM LEADER: Coordinate, track and delegate inventory control procedures to meet regular deadlines of inventory management. Complete required training and cross-train to support business needs and team members' development.
Supervisor: Joshua Goins (850-543-0123)
Okay to contact this Supervisor: Yes

Florida State University Panama City Campus
4750 Collegiate Drive
Panama City, FL 32405 United States

01/20xx - 05/20xx
Salary: 10.00 USD Per Hour
Hours per week: 10

This resume is an excerpt of a resume created in the USAJOBS builder to show you what a resume looks like when printed from USAJOBS.

Representative for Student Government Council
Duties, Accomplishments and Related Skills:
STUDENT REPRESENTATIVE AND ADVOCATE: Represented students' interests as part of
the Student Government Council. Received comments, feedback and grievances from
students; discussed courses of action with fellow council members and recommended
actions to University leadership. Held office hours to address student concerns and
represented student government at events. Prepared and presented reports to council.

ADMINISTRATION/RECORD-KEEPING: Maintained records of student government
complaints, appeals, and grievances from candidates. Provided any necessary assistance.

ELECTIONS CHAIR: Oversaw the voting system for Fall and Spring semesters. Received
the candidates' packets and advised them on election procedures at the candidate
information meeting. Provided guidance to the candidates on by-laws. Reviewed by-laws
and submitted proposals, and made recommendations to the leadership council.
Supervisor: Elaine Keller (850-543-2121)
Okay to contact this Supervisor: Yes

Naval Surface Center Panama City
101 Vernon Avenue
Panama City Beach, FL   32407 United States

07/20xx - 10/20xx   **Series:** 0303 **Pay**
Hours per week: 40   **Plan:** NG **Grade:** 1
Assistant (This is a federal job)
Duties, Accomplishments and Related Skills:
ENTERPRISE RESOURCE DATABASE UPDATES: Entered purchase requests into
automated Enterprise Resource Planning database for all Navy departments at NSWC
Panama City, including small purchase card orders, government supply orders, and
contracts for labor and materials.

RECORDS AND PURCHASE ORDER MANAGEMENT: Created routine purchase requisitions
(PR) and tracked purchase orders to ensure materials and services were delivered as
requested. Reviewed requests and entered information; researched missing or incorrect
information. Verified and ensured correct data entry, coding and forms. Provided end
users with feedback to ensure on-time delivery of materials/services. Helped resolve
error rate associated with inaccurate purchase requests.

MAINTAINING CLASSIFIED RECORDS: Diligently managed purchase requests for
classified projects. Securely filed and entered records concerning classified purchases.

COMPUTER SKILLS: Utilized Microsoft Word, Excel and internal databases to maintain
purchase orders, research information and research references for purchasing materials.
Communicated with subject matter experts on issues not covered by reference materials.
Used oral and written communication skills to resolve issues. Created and maintained file
system to maintain PR documents generated.

KEY ACCOMPLISHMENT
• Navy had a daily goal of 50-80 purchases inputted into Milstrip. On average, I created
77 purchase orders for Milstrip and P-Cards with a 94 percent approval rate.
Supervisor: Shelia Cox (850-234-4713)
Okay to contact this Supervisor: Yes

USAJOBS Application Tracking

Application Package Status: See Details Tab

Job Title: INVENTORY MANAGEMENT SPECIALIST

Vacancy Identification Number: 1026916

Announcement Number: 9S-TRANS-1026916-038368-MAF

USAJOBS Control Number: 358913500

Applicant: KATHRYN K TROUTMAN

Closing Date: Thursday, January 16, 2014

Contact: AFPC RSC - (800)525-0102

[Change My Answers] [Add Documents] [Update Biographic Information] [View/Print My Answers]

Most information below pertains to the most recent version of your Application Package. (Explain This.)

Notice to Applicants: Please ensure you keep copies of all documents you uploaded or faxed, including your resume, as well as any notifications sent to you. They will be deleted from the system after 3 years of the closing date of the announcement.

| Details | Checklist |

Assessments

Status	Name	Date Submitted	Due Date
Complete	Assessment Questionnaire	1/16/2014 2:36:29 PM	
Complete	Assessment Questionnaire	1/16/2014 2:36:29 PM	

Documents

* Security Alert: Protect your privacy

	Status	Document Type	Source	Re-Use Document	Date Received	Original File Name
View	Processed	Resume	USAJOBS		01/16/2014 02:31 PM	
	Not Received	Cover Letter				
	Not Received	DD-214				
	Not Received	Other				
	Not Received	Other Veterans Document				

Messages

	Message Type	Date Emailed	Date Printed
View	Notice of Results (NORs)	1/18/2014 1:27:48 AM	
View	Notification Letter	1/21/2014 4:12:24 PM	
View	Acknowledgement Letter	1/16/2014 2:36:29 PM	

Application Processing Status

	Status	Date Submitted

Notice of Results (NOR) gives you information about the status of your application. The types of responses could be: Not Eligible, Eligible, Best Qualified, Best Qualified and Not Among the Most Qualified to be Referred, Best Qualified and Referred. It's important to check your NORs, so that you can gauge the success of your applications.

You can find your Notice of Results in Applicationmanager.gov under My Application Packages. You may also receive your results by email, or you may contact the HR representative listed in the announcement to find out what happened with your application.

Automated Email fromHR | **RESULT: EL (Eligible) for GS-05/07**

This refers to the application you recently submitted to this office for the position below:

Position Title: Health Insurance Specialist
Series/Grade: 0107-13
Hiring Office: Center for Medicaid and CHIP Services CMCS
Spec Title: Health Insurance Specialist
Grade: 13
Rating: EL

Referral Type: Open to all qualified candidates
Referral Name: AJU-14-MSt-02039S0
Status: NR - Not Referred

_____

Status Code: Status Message:
NR - Not   We have reviewed your application and found you eligible for the position listed above
Referred   Status code. However, you were not among the most highly qualified candidates. Therefore, your name will not be referred to the employing agency at this time.
Rating Code: Rating Message:
EL   You are eligible for this specialty and grade.

Email from HR | **RESULT: Conditional Offer of Employment**

Subject: Tentative Selection Notification: CBP Technician, GS-1802-05, Eastport ID

This email is to extend a conditional offer of employment to you for the following position:
Job Title: CBP Technician
Payplan/Job Series/Grade/Step: GS-1802-05 Step 01
Full Performance Level: GS-07

We are making this conditional offer of employment based on a projection of hiring needs, the existence of a vacant funded position, the absence of any hiring restrictions, and any other controlling factors.

STRATEGY 8

Give Yourself All the Credit You Can on the Questionnaire

DO NOT make the most common mistakes on your questionnaire answers

- ❯ **Don't deflate your score.**

- ❯ This is a TEST! You need to get 85 to 95% to get best qualified

- ❯ Always PREVIEW the questionnaire before applying

- ❯ Give yourself all the credit you can.

- ❯ Make sure the resume matches the questionnaire.

Sample Self-Assessment Questionnaire

Sample Questionnaire: New Orleans Jazz Musician!

This job announcement and the questionnaire is highly-specialized. For this NPS Park Ranger (Interpretation), they are seeking an individual who can provide informational and interpretive talks specializing in knowledge and experience in jazz music in New Orleans. The questionnaire is also asking for the ability to "perform jazz music, instrumentally or vocally, during interpretive presentations." The questionnaire is also asking for expertise in New Orleans traditions that feature jazz, brass band parading traditions, places where early jazz was performed in New Orleans, social aid and pleasure clubs, the diversity and/or stories of people who created jazz in New Orleans.

TIP: If you are not a jazz performer and an expert in New Orleans jazz "pleasure clubs," do not apply for this job.

Park Ranger (Interpretation) GS-0025-09

KSA-1. Ability to research, develop and present interpretive talks and demonstrations for diverse audiences.

For the task statements below, please select from A through E to indicate the skill level that you possess for each task listed. The task statements were developed based on the knowledge, skills, abilities, and competencies needed to perform the work of this position. It is important that your application package, including a resume or application form, clearly shows how you possess the experience and skills levels you claim in this questionnaire. Each of your responses must be clearly supported by your education, training, and/or specific work experience you describe in your application packet submitted for this position (application form or resume, transcripts, list and description of training completed and/or other items you submit). If not, your score will be lowered or you will be found not qualified. The information you provide will be verified. Any exaggeration of your experience, false statements, or attempts to conceal information may be grounds for rating you ineligible, not hiring you, or for firing you after you begin work.

A- I am regarded as an expert in performing this task, or I have trained others (or am consulted by others) on how to do it.

B- I have performed this task as a regular part of my job, independently and usually without supervision from a senior employee.

C- I have performed this task on the job, with close supervision from a supervisor or senior employee.

D- I have had education or training performing this task, but I have not yet performed it on the job.

E- I have not had education, training or experience performing this task.

2. Present informational and interpretive talks and/or guided tours to visitors (individuals, groups, and special interest groups) to enhance the public's understanding and enjoyment of jazz music in New Orleans.

3. Perform jazz music, instrumentally or vocally, during interpretive presentations for the public and school programs.

4. Express information on cultural resources to diverse audiences, effectively taking into account the audience and nature of the information.

5. Provide guidance to others in developing interpretive programs.

6. Plan, develop and present interpretive presentations following the principles of the Interpretive Development Program (IDP).

7. Research and develop original illustrated programs, walks, and musical demonstrations that feature cultural resource topics such as; New Orleans traditions that feature jazz, brass band parading traditions, places where early jazz was performed in New Orleans, social aid & pleasure clubs, the diversity and or stories of people who created jazz in New Orleans.

8. Use a variety of presentation techniques in making presentations, such as storytelling, hands-on, musical demonstrations, questioning, etc. (Be sure to list and describe these in your application materials.)

9. Make interpretive presentations that incorporate and reflect and a variety of learning styles (such as audio, visual, and/or kinesthetic/interactive learning styles).

10. Facilitate the opportunity for visitors to make meaningful, personal connections with park resources (tangibles) using thematic interpretation that incorporates intangible meanings and universal concepts.

11. Conduct research and prepare outlines and written materials to develop interpretive programs. (Research methods can include interviews, literature, library research, and/or other means of investigation).

12. Research and develop interpretive programs and materials on the roots of jazz.

13. Research and develop interpretive programs and materials on the early development of jazz in New Orleans.

14. Research and develop interpretive programs and materials on the progression of jazz.

KSA-2. Ability to manage all aspects of a high quality interpretive program.

15. Perform staff duties such as supervising, training, coaching and mentoring interpretive staff and volunteers. (Please specifically describe your experience in your application).

16. Provide constructive advice based on the NPS Interpretive Development Program or similar criteria, and mentor volunteer and seasonal employee performance.

17. Create a positive work environment.

KSA-3. Ability to communicate effectively with visitors and representatives of external groups such as park partners, neighboring communities, agencies, etc.

18. Serve as a front-line representative of an organization; answering questions; and responding to comments, concerns, problems and/or complaints following established guidelines.

19. Work independently handling public relations and/or other issues under stressful or controversial situations.

20. Build and maintain cooperative working relationships with park partners (Please specifically describe this experience in your application).

21. Maintain courtesy and rapport with individuals and groups when contacting them to gain their cooperation (e.g., when contacting individuals or groups who are behaving in an unsafe way, or are not in compliance with rules, in order to obtain their compliance.)

22. Serve as a team leader with a diverse group of partners to achieve park goals.

KSA-4. Ability to communicate orally and in writing.

23. Communicate professionally via radio, TV, social media, and through the park's website.

24. Present information to the public in writing. (Please specifically describe this experience in your application).

25. Prepare correspondence in reply to written inquiries and communications.

26. Gather information and prepare articles, publications, and contribute to the park's social media efforts.

27. Write bulletins, brochures, or articles on natural, cultural or historic resource topics. (Be sure to list and describe in your application materials.)

28. Prepare technical or program reports.

29. Write narrative text for public displays or exhibits.

30. As previously explained, your ratings in this Occupational Questionnaire are subject to evaluation and verification based on the documents and references you submit.

PART TWO
Special Insights for Specific Jobseekers

Information Technology Specialist

Acquisition Professional

Management and Program Analyst

Career Change Resumes

GS-2210

Information Technology Specialist

Writing a resume for the IT world has some interesting challenges, whether the resume targets a job in private industry or the federal government. On the one hand, you want to impress the reader with your technical expertise, and what better way to do that than to use lots of technical jargon (appropriately, of course)? On the other hand, your resume will likely also be read by a variety of nontechnical personnel, from the junior human resources specialist logging in the resume or performing an initial screening, all the way to the hiring manager, who may or may not have a technical background. How can you satisfy both of these audiences, plus position yourself as "Best Qualified" for the position you want?

That's the purpose of this chapter: to help you first of all to understand the types of IT jobs available in the federal world so that you can do a good job of the most important step—selecting those positions that are the best matches for your career aspirations and experience—and then knowing how to present your IT education, training, and job experience in an effective marketing format that produces results.

The most interesting trend in federal IT jobs is that more and more, the government is taking its lead from industry. In all areas, government managers are challenged to think like entrepreneurs, to focus on the bottom line, and to build standard, repeatable business processes based on industry-wide best practices. Always remember when developing your federal resume, your cover letter, and any other component of your application package, that IT systems and software are never the end goal; they are merely the tools to build successful, mission-driven business systems. Every job duty and accomplishment you describe should maintain that focus. What does this mean in the IT arena? Look to the key business drivers in the IT industry and you will find the federal government in lockstep.

Industry Certifications

IT positions in both the government and industry increasingly require industry certifications. Those most in demand include the following:

- **Microsoft:** Microsoft certifications, which demonstrate your knowledge of Microsoft products, are still highly in demand. Microsoft has revamped their certification program, which now includes three major tiers: MCSA (Microsoft Certified Solutions Associate), MCSE (Microsoft Certified Solutions Expert), and MCSD (Microsoft Certified Solutions Developer). In addition, the certifications are further subdivided into function (Server, Desktop, Database, and Developer). For instance, one of the MSCE certifications is MSCE: Desktop Infrastructure. As you are probably aware, cloud technologies are a very hot topic in the IT world right now, and the MSCE: Private Cloud certification would be a great ticket for that career path. Note that MCSE requires recertification every 3 years and MCSD requires recertification every 2 years. Microsoft offers many other certifications from entry level (Microsoft Certified Professional (MCP)) to expert. You can find out more details regarding Microsoft certifications at www.microsoft.com/learning.

- **CompTIA:** The Computing Technology Industry Association (CompTIA) also provides a broad range of vendor neutral IT certifications, starting with the A+, Network +, and Security+ certifications, which require recertification every 3 years. You can learn more about these certifications, and the many others provided by CompTIA, at certification.comptia.org.

- **IT Security:** CISSP (Certified Information Systems Security Professional) is probably the most in-demand ("gold standard") certification in the market; however, there are multiple other IT security certifications you should investigate, including:

CompTIA Security+; Global Information Assurance Certification (GIAC) Security Essentials; Certified Ethical Hacker (CEH); and Certified Information Security Manager (CISM). You can learn more about GIAC certifications, which require recertification every 4 years, at www.giac.org/certifications. CEH certification is offered by the EC-Council (www.eccouncil.org). CISM is offered by the Information Systems Audit and Control Association (ISACA)—see www.isaca.org—and the CISSP is governed by the International Information Systems Security Certification Consortium, also known as (ISC)² (www.isc2.org). Given the ever-present security threat to enterprise systems and data assets, if you have an IT security credential, you probably will have a job!

❯ **VMWare:** Another hot area in the computer industry is virtual computing platforms, and the industry leader in virtualization is VMware, which offers multiple certifications in its product set, including the VMWare Certified Professional (VCP). Like Microsoft, VMWare provides multiple levels and categories of certifications. Take a look at mylearn.vmware.com to check out their certification paths.

❯ **Cisco:** Cisco continues to be an industry leader in networking solutions, and also provides multiple certifications, which again have multiple levels (Entry, Associate, Professional, Expert and Architect) and multiple categories. Achieving a Cisco Certified Network Associate (CCNA), Cisco Certified Network Professional (CCNP), Cisco Certified Design Associate (CCDA), or Cisco Certified Design Expert (CCDE) certification will demonstrate your expertise with Cisco technologies. You can locate further details at www.cisco.com (search for training or certification).

❯ **PMI:** The Project Management Institute (PMI) (www.pmi.org) has become the standard for project management best practices for the federal government as well as for private industry. Government contracts frequently require that the Project Manager be either PMI certified as a Project Management Professional (PMP) or have a Defense Acquisition Workforce Improvement Act (DAWIA) certification (available only as a government employee), particularly for any IT position that includes IT acquisitions. The PMP credential requires not only 35 hours of training and passing a certification test, but also 4500 hours of demonstrated project management experience (if you have a 4-year degree; 7500 hours without a 4-year degree). There are also continuing education requirements, requiring you to complete 60 PDUs (Professional Development Units) every 3 years. Related disciplines that you should stress in your resume include Risk Management, Configuration Management, Earned Value Management, Quality Assurance, and Communications Management.

- **ITIL:** Information Technology Infrastructure Library (itlibrary.org). This is actually an IT service delivery standard derived from the British government. While PMI focuses generically on project management issues across any industry, this is increasingly becoming PMI's IT companion. ITIL brings together many of the disciplines you have come to know in the IT world: Problem Management, Configuration Management, Release Management, and IT Service Delivery. Again, there are several levels of certification—the original Foundation, Practitioners, and Managers certificates have now been transitioned to Foundation, Intermediate, Expert, and Master certifications. Check out www.axelos.com for further details on this IT service management approach and its associated certifications. You should reference any and all of these disciplines and terms in your resume materials if you have this type of experience.

- **CMM/CMMI:** Capability Maturity Model (CMM) and Capability Maturity Model Integration (CMMI) are process-improvement standards developed and fostered by the Carnegie Mellon Software Engineering Institute (SEI). The federal government is increasingly pushing for both its own organizations and contractors to implement best practices for process management that are validated in a CMM or CMMI rating. Although this is really an organizational certification, any training or experience you have in assisting your firm or client to gain a CMM/CMMI rating should be highlighted. Read more at cmmiinstitute.com.

- **Other Certifications:** There is certainly a wealth of other highly regarded certifications in the IT world, from Amazon Web Services (AWS) Certified Solutions Architect to Lean Six Sigma to Open Group Master Architect. Just a quick search under "highest paying certifications" or "hottest IT certifications" should provide sufficient information to jumpstart your IT professional education.

If you have one of these or other certifications, you definitely will want to highlight this in the first half of the first page of your federal resume. If you do not have any certifications, there is no time like the present to get started. Although formal training is important, you can get started on many of these certifications through self-study, and the time and cost invested will be well paid back.

Cyber Security

The news highlights the continued threats to both national and corporate IT infrastructures and data assets from cyber attack. Strengthening our defenses in this area will continue to be one of the top priorities for the federal government. The **Comprehensive National Cybersecurity Initiative (CNCI)**, launched by President George W. Bush in 2008 in National Security Presidential Directive 54/Homeland Security Presidential Directive 23 (NSPD-54/HSPD-23), established the nation's goals in defending against these threats. Take a look at the White House webpage on cyber security (https://www.whitehouse.gov/issues/foreign-policy/cybersecurity) for a description of the multiple initiatives underway to secure the nation in Cyberspace under CNCI. Also become familiar with the **Federal Information Security Management Act of 2002 (FISMA)**, which requires each federal agency to establish an agency-wide, risk-based information security program. For more details, see http://csrc.nist.gov/groups/SMA/fisma/.

Enterprise Architectures

Both industry and government have realized that reinventing the wheel again and again is neither fiscally nor mission responsible. Many job positions posted by the federal government are derived from federal-wide initiatives to design "reusable," "interoperable," "accessible," "scalable," "enterprise" systems and solutions. Start by taking a look at the website for the Office of E-Government and Information Technology (https://www.whitehouse.gov/omb/e-gov) as well as the Federal Enterprise Architecture website (https://www.whitehouse.gov/omb/e-gov/FEA), which provide links to the key documents guiding the federal government's approach to developing and using Enterprise Architectures, with the goals of streamlining citizen access to federal government agencies and saving taxpayer dollars.

Cloud Technologies

Another key driver in the 21st Century has been the phenomenon of "moving to the cloud," and the federal government has been no exception. In layman's terms, this move to cloud technologies means that federal agencies are required to first consider using shared data and computing resources before they go out to purchase or develop their own hardware and software. Cloud computing takes advantage of virtualization, which implements a layer of "virtual" systems on top of the physical system, enabling the capability to dynamically allocate resources based on demand. Driven by industry giants like Google and Amazon, the industry has moved toward several new service models, including Infrastructure as a Service (IaaS), Software as a Service (SaaS), and Platform as a Service (PaaS). Again, consult the White House E-Gov website (https://www.whitehouse.gov/omb/e-gov/strategiesandguides) for links to the key documents guiding similar efforts in the federal government.

Systems Development Life Cycle (SDLC)

The government has learned the lesson that the real cost for a system is the total life-cycle cost—from product or system inception through development, testing, acceptance, implementation, and then life-cycle support and even decommissioning. If you are a software developer or hardware integrator, or even plan, acquire, and then implement new systems, you have had to consider all of these life-cycle aspects. Again, incorporating the appropriate and accepted terms for this experience into your resume demonstrates your expertise and awareness of these imperatives on the IT industry and federal IT initiatives.

Continuity of Operations (COOP)

Continuity of Operations (COOP) and Disaster Recovery Planning have been high on the federal government's to-do list since 9/11. One place to start is by consulting FEMA's Federal Preparedness Circular (FPC) 65 (www.fas.org/irp/offdocs/pdd/fpc-65.htm). It is very likely that you will have played some role in disaster preparedness in any IT position in which you have served. Highlighting this experience and relating it to the term "COOP" will ring true to the hiring manager for almost all positions.

Business Process Reengineering (BPR)

Remember the focus on documented, repeatable business processes? The buzzword in the business world for developing these is Business Process Reengineering (BPR). If you have been around awhile in the IT world, you have at some point had to think about how you currently manage a process (the "as-is" scenario) and how you could improve it in the future (the "to-be" process). If you have led or participated on projects to map processes like this, you have essentially been involved in BPR (and should take credit for it and use the correct term).

IT Planning and Acquisition

Whether you have formally served as a Contracting Officer's Technical Representative (COTR) in the federal government, as a Project Manager for a government project, or even researched, recommended, and documented requirements for IT items or services to be procured, this is one area that you should definitely highlight. Become familiar with terms such as Statement of Work (SOW), Statement of Objectives (SOO), and Request for Proposals (RFP). Even for private industry experience, try to cast your expertise in these terms.

You should also educate yourself on the **Clinger-Cohen Act of 1996** or the **Information Technology Management Reform Act (ITMRA)**, which required the federal government to reform the acquisition, management, and disposal of its IT resources to better enable agencies to keep up with the high pace of technology change. Clinger-Cohen implemented an IT planning process called **Capital Planning and Investment Control (CPIC)** and placed the responsibility for IT planning in each agency under a Chief Information Officer (CIO), with the Office of Management and Budget (OMB) at the center of the process. CPIC requires each agency to follow a disciplined IT planning process aligned with its Enterprise Architecture. Key documents related to this process include:

- OMB Circular A-130, Management of Federal Information Resources, which establishes policies for the management of federal information resources (https://www.whitehouse.gov/omb/circulars_a130_a130trans4/).

- OMB Exhibit 300, submitted by each federal agency to justify each request for a major IT investment.

- OMB Exhibit 53, submitted annually by each federal agency to report its budget estimates for its IT investment portfolio.

How the Federal Government **Has Organized IT Positions**

The first step in conducting an effective job search for IT positions in the federal government is to understand the various job series that apply to IT-related positions (see www.opm.gov/fedclass and select Classifying General Schedule Positions and then Position Classification Standards under Classifying White Collar Positions). Searching via the Occupational Series/Job Categories on USAJOBS (www. usajobs. gov) is essential in identifying vacancies compatible with your education and experience.

Jobs in Series GS-2210 and Beyond

If you type in "Information Technology" in the "Occupational Series or Job Category" field in the USAJOBS Advanced Search feature, you will see all of the available IT job series, 2200 ("2200" is the Job Series; "Information Technology" is the Job Category). The overall Information Technology job series is 2200; however, the vast majority of posted jobs are in the 2210 series, Information Technology Management. The Position Classification Standard[1] defines the 2210 series as follows:

❯ GS-2210, Information Technology Management: "This series covers two-grade interval administrative positions that manage, supervise, lead, administer, develop, deliver, and support information technology (IT) systems and services. This series covers only those positions for which the paramount requirement is knowledge of IT principles, concepts, and methods; e.g., data storage, software applications, networking."

Note, however, that there are a few other job series of interest depending on the type of job you are seeking:

❯ GS-2299, Information Technology Student Trainee: These positions do not refer to the temporary, summer job types of employment, but for "student trainee positions made under career-conditional or career appointments in the competitive service. A student may be appointed to any position that leads to qualification in a two-grade interval professional, administrative, or technical occupational series, and that provides an opportunity for the student's growth and development toward the target position."

❯ GS-0332, Computer Operations Series: This series covers positions where the primary duties involve "operating or supervising the operations of the controls of the digital computer system." If you have experience as a Computer Operator, you

---

1   All Job Series Definitions found on www.opm.gov/policy-data-oversight/classification-qualifications/classifying-general-schedule-positions/#url=Standards

might want to check positions in this category as well as in GS-2210.

❯ GS-0335, Computer Clerk and Assistant Series: This series is closely aligned with GS-0332 in that it focuses on providing a clerical level of data-processing support. Sample duties as a Computer Assistant might be installing new desktop systems, issuing data media, maintaining system documentation, and receiving and resolving routine user trouble calls.

❯ GS-0854, Computer Engineering Series: These Computer Engineering positions are characterized as "professional" positions requiring extensive academic qualifications in computer hardware, software, and system architectures. The work revolves around the "research, design, development, testing, evaluation, and maintenance of computer hardware and systems software in an integrated manner." Sample positions might involve developing computer simulations or leading the design and integration of complex IT systems.

❯ GS-1550, Computer Science Series: This is the most scientifically oriented type of IT work and would typically require advanced degrees and skills in computer science, engineering, statistics, and mathematics, and involve "research into computer science methods and techniques."

More Details on the GS-2210 Series

The Office of Personnel Management (OPM) Job Family Classification Standard for Administrative Work in the Information Technology Group, GS-2200 (www.opm. gov/policy-data-oversight/classification-qualifications/classifying-general-schedule-positions/standards/2200/gs2200a.pdf) fully defines the Information Technology Job Series. Note that the 2210 series is considered an "administrative" position as opposed to a "clerical or professional" position. A professional series generally requires a specific educational level. For example, GS-1550 (Computer Science) and GS-0854 (Computer Engineer) are considered professional series because they require a body of knowledge related to math and science (essentially a college degree with courses taken in math, engineering, statistics, or computer science). Because the 2210 is an administrative series, people who come into a GS-2210-05 position, with the promotion potential of GS-2210-11, have the possibility of being promoted to GS-7/9/11 (two grades at a time). After reaching GS-11, the promotions are limited to one grade at a time (to GS-12/13/14/15).

The GS-2210 series includes but is not limited to the 11 Specialty Titles, often called Parenthetical Titles, included in Table 15.1. Note the specialty abbreviation that is often included in the job title in the position description.

Descriptions taken from *Descriptions for the GS-2200 Occupational Series*,
www.opm.gov/policy-data-oversight/classification-qualifications/classifying-general-
schedule-positions/standards/2200/gs2200a.pdf

GS-2200 Specialty	Description
Applications Software (APPSW)	Work that involves the design, documentation, development, modification, testing, installation, implementation, and support of new or existing applications software.
Operating Systems (OS)	Work that involves the planning, installation, configuration, testing, implementation, and management of the systems environment in support of the organization's IT architecture and business needs.
Network Services (NETWORK)	Work that involves the planning, analysis, design, development, testing, quality assurance, configuration, installation, implementation, integration, maintenance, and/or management of networked systems used for the transmission of information in voice, data, and/or video formats.
Data Management (DATAMGT)	Work that involves the planning, development, implementation, and administration of systems for the acquisition, storage, and retrieval of data.
Internet (INET)	Work that involves the technical planning, design, development, testing, implementation, and management of Internet, intranet, and extranet activities, including systems/applications development and technical management of websites. This specialty includes only positions that require the application of technical knowledge of Internet systems, services, and technologies.
Systems Administration (SYSADMIN)	Work that involves planning and coordinating the installation, testing, operation, troubleshooting, and maintenance of hardware
Customer Support (CUSTSPT)	Work that involves the planning and delivery of customer support services, including installation, configuration, troubleshooting, customer assistance, and/or training, in response to customer requirements.

Descriptions for the **GS-2210 Series**

Grades for Occupations in the GS-2210 Series

Occupations	Grades
2210 Information Technology Management Series	9, 11, 12, 13, 14, 15
0855 Electronics Engineering Series	12, 13, 14, 15
0854 Computer Engineering Series	12, 13, 14, 15
0391 Telecommunications Series	9, 11, 12, 13

Cybersecurity Competencies for the GS-2210-12

Technical Competencies

- Communications security management
- Compliance
- Computer network defense
- Configuration management
- Information assurance
- Information systems/ network security
- Information systems security certification
- Operating systems
- Security

General Competencies

- Accountability
- Attention to detail
- Computer skills
- Customer service
- Decision making
- Flexibility
- Integrity/honesty
- Interpersonal skills
- Learning
- Memory
- Oral communication
- Problem solving
- Reading
- Reasoning
- Resilience
- Self-management
- Stress tolerance
- Teamwork
- Technical competence
- Writing

Selecting the Right Job Announcement for You

Selecting the right job announcement in the first place is just as critical for IT positions as for any other position in your job search. No matter how good your resume materials are, if you truly do not have the credentials required by the hiring manager, it is close to certain that you will not be in the Best Qualified range. So how can you tell from reading an IT job announcement whether you might be minimally qualified or seriously at the top of the pack?

Analyzing a Sample Announcement

Let's take a sample IT job announcement and really look at it. Here is an actual (but abbreviated) job announcement for an Information Security Specialist at the GS-11 level. Table 15.3 presents each sentence from the vacancy announcement and the skills required for the job, and an interpretation of the requirement for this skill.

IT Specialist (APPSW), GS-2210-11

DUTIES

- Provides broad technical and professional support involving analyzing, diagnosing, and recovery of system abnormal ends; developing, testing, and coding of mainframe jobs and production libraries to reflect system change request.
- Maintains, controls, and updates test environment with new, current, and proposed changes for the joint payroll software. Updates job schedules using Control-M or other mainframe/mid-tier scheduling packages.
- Responsible for the development of system documentation such as maintenance manuals, tests and implementation plans, specification documents and/or database feasibility studies.
- Monitors and reports on the status and progress of work, checks on work in progress, and reviews completed work for compliance with supervisor's priorities, methods, deadlines and instructions.

Specialized Experience is defined as: experience in Job Control Language (JCL); using scheduling tools such as Control-M and other mainframe tools; analyzing system change requests to assess impact on test or production environments; documenting and communicating system issues and risks related to a mainframe payroll system; preparing test plans, executing test scripts; and providing customer service support both internally and externally.

The first thing you should do is to copy all of the information in the announcement that describes the job itself into a Word document. Be sure to look at all pertinent sections of the announcement—Job Summary, Duties, Qualifications Required, Specialized Experience, as well as the Occupational Questionnaire. For this exercise, ONLY copy in the material that describes the job itself (as opposed to eligibility, travel, security clearance, educational requirements, etc). Now, make each sentence and/or skill a SEPARATE BULLET. And lastly, go through and reorganize all the bullets so that similar tasks or skills are together. Just doing this exercise will force you to think through the key categories of skills they are looking for. Those "categories" are the KEYWORDS that you will want to consider to use in your federal resume, they are also crucial in determining if you are truly qualified for the position.

TRANSFORMED, this might look like below. Note that there is no one perfect analysis, and some bullets might actually fit under two categories or KEYWORDS.

TECHNICAL SUPPORT
- Provides broad technical and professional support involving analyzing, diagnosing, and recovery of system abnormal ends.

DOCUMENTATION/COMMUNICATIONS
- Responsible for the development of system documentation such as maintenance manuals, tests and implementation plans, specification documents and/or database feasibility studies.
- Documenting and communicating system issues and risks related to a mainframe payroll system.
- Monitors and reports on the status and progress of work, checks on work in progress, and reviews completed work for compliance with supervisor's priorities, methods, deadlines and instructions.

JOB CONTROL
- Experience in Job Control Language (JCL).
- Updates job schedules using Control-M or other mainframe/mid-tier scheduling packages.
- Using scheduling tools such as Control-M and other mainframe tools.

CHANGE MANAGEMENT
- Analyzing system change requests to assess impact on test or production environments.
- Maintains, controls, and updates test environment with new, current, and proposed changes for the joint payroll software.

SOFTWARE DEVELOPMENT/TESTING
- Developing, testing, and coding of mainframe jobs and production libraries to reflect system change request.
- Preparing test plans.
- Executing test scripts.

CUSTOMER SERVICE
- Providing customer service support both internally and externally.

The next step is to cross-check your experience, and your resume, against each area required in the job announcement. At some level, this analysis will involve a judgment call as to whether the requirement is a clear, hard requirement (you must have experience in this very explicit application or system in order to qualify) or a more generalized skill that could be satisfied from a somewhat different context.

Analyzing Required Skills for an IT Specialist Position

Looking at the IT Specialist (APPSW) position, let's categorize each skill area described in the announcement:

Job Requirement	Interpretation
TECHNICAL SUPPORT	This is a fairly general statement regarding providing support for abnormal system/software crashes. As long as you have technical experience troubleshooting bugs and crashes for software systems, you should qualify for this requirement.
DOCUMENTATION/ COMMUNICATION	This group of requirements has some generalities but also one specific requirement. **Specific Requirement** – You must have experience with mainframe payroll systems. **General Requirements** – You should also be able to demonstrate that you have developed some forms of system documentation, studies, or plans, and that you have reported on work status in order to meet requirements and deadlines. This could likely be satisfied from a variety of job experience.
JOB CONTROL	The requirements for this area are all pretty specific. **Specific Requirements** – You must have experience with JCL, Control-M or another mainframe scheduling tool.
CHANGE MANAGEMENT	There are specific requirements reflected in this area: **Specific Requirements** – You must have had experience implementing changes related to a change management process, plus you should have experience testing proposed changes in a test environment. **General Requirements** – You should be able to demonstrate that you have tracked and implemented software changes in a controlled fashion. This requirement could possibly be met outside of a payroll software environment.
SOFTWARE DEVELOPMENT/ TESTING	There are some very specific requirements also in this area: **Specific Requirements** – You must have development and testing experience on a mainframe and should specifically mention preparing and executing test plans and test scripts.
CUSTOMER SERVICE	Again, this is a fairly broad statement; as long as you can demonstrate that you have personally provided customer service, you should be able to meet this requirement.

Summarizing Table 15.3, to have a strong chance to qualify for this position, you must have solid experience with the following:

- Development and testing experience for a payroll system in a mainframe environment.

- Experience with JCL and some type of mainframe scheduling tool (Control-M or other).

- Experience managing changes in a structured Change Management process.

- Experience testing proposed changes in a test environment.

- Hopefully you also have good customer service skills as well as experience developing documentation and managing projects.

The best part about this method is that once you have analyzed the job announcement, you are in a great position to determine if you truly qualify for the position, and if so, you are now ready to rework your resume to meet this outline of the job requirements. Using the KEYWORDs you selected during your analysis, include a description that highlights what you have done in each job for each of the areas that apply to that experience. Also work to compile a list of specific accomplishments that can be closely aligned to these key job requirements. NOTE: If after this type of analysis, you find that you really do not have one of the key required skills, it is highly unlikely that you would ultimately be selected for the position. It would be a better use of your time and effort to keep looking for a better match.

When You Don't Match the Requirements Exactly

The toughest call is when the announcement mentions a specific government application or system that you could have used only if you were already in that job or agency. In this case, consider several factors, including the exact language used (is this required, or desirable?) as well as the overall announcement itself. If there is one position and the posting time is short, the requirement is probably very firm. If there are multiple positions available, you might have a better chance of gaining an interview even if your experience is missing one of the requirements.

The real danger, especially for the applicant coming in from outside the federal government, is that you might assume that an unfamiliar term such as "certification and accreditation" is just a generic description of the process of putting into place a robust plan to manage information technology security threats. In actuality, Certification and Accreditation (C&A) is often capitalized and refers to a very formalized process within the federal government of identifying, prioritizing, and putting into place appropriate controls for all of the potential risks associated with bringing a new system or network into production. Although different federal agencies may follow different standards and processes (a good example is the National Institute of Standards and Technology Risk Management Framework (NIST RMF)), it is generally safe to say that agencies as a general rule have fairly formalized requirements in this area.

The ideal approach, of course, would be to speak with someone in a similar technical environment to ensure that you fully understand the requirements. Don't hesitate to use any technical contacts you have to look over the job announcement with you if you see any terms that you are not 100 percent certain you understand. As with any position, you can also call the Point of Contact provided with the announcement to better understand what the agency is looking for.

Frequently Asked Questions about **IT Resumes**

This chapter assumes that you already know the basics of putting together your federal resume, and that you have done the job analysis to identify the key knowledge, skills, abilities, and experience you need to highlight to be fully qualified for the target positions.

Here, then, are some recommendations and answers to common questions about putting together a really effective IT resume. Remember that every IT job seeker's specific experience and situation will be different, and this, plus the specifics of the job you are applying for, needs to be taken into account in the final format, organization, and content of your resume. So take these as good rules of thumb, but also feel free to apply a different strategy if it makes sense for your particular situation.

Where should I put my certification?
Certifications are as important for federal IT positions as they are increasingly in private industry. Don't bury them on the last page. These belong near the top of the first page, such as after the Profile and any Clearance you may have.

Where should I put my clearance(s)?
Security clearances are tremendously important in the current job environment. If you have or have ever had a clearance, you should note this right after your Profile. Include dates and whether the clearance is still current. Even the fact that you have an expired clearance could be an asset in that the hiring manager might feel you would pass a new background investigation.

Where and how should I list all of the hardware/software I have worked with?
This is a tough one, and it really depends on just how hands-on the target position is and whether you have really impressive achievements that will take up lots of real estate on the first page of the resume. The rule of thumb: If you are very hands-on in your position—a system administrator, software developer, or systems integrator— you should probably provide a categorized list of your key technical skill areas at the bottom of page 1. If you currently work more as a project manager or supervisor, devote the first page more to your expertise and significant accomplishments and save the technical skills for the last page.

Another hint: Be sure to wipe out all the outdated technologies from your resume. Nothing looks more dated than including references to Wang, Windows for Workgroups, Windows 9x, and COBOL (unless, of course, you are actually applying for a COBOL position if there is one still lurking out there somewhere). Even "client/ server" at this point sounds pretty out-of-date in a web-centric world.

One more note: Avoid the obvious. Don't drill down to the point that you are listing every single version of software you have ever used or every printer you ever touched. Suffice it to say that you have worked on Tektronix printers, Cisco routers, or Dell servers.

Should I only include hardware/software on which I am an expert?

You should not limit your Computer Expertise section to just those hardware and software components where you feel you are expert. But certainly, do not list items you have just "heard of" of or "studied." It is appropriate to list hardware and software that you actually had to use, install, or support in the performance of your job duties (or in completing academic projects).

I am a contractor to a specific federal agency. How do I indicate that in my resume?

Be very careful here. As a contractor, you need to list your contracting firm employer as your employer. Never imply that you worked for an agency if you were not a federal employee.

Instead, include the agency's name either in your job description ("Provided contracted system administration support for XYZ Agency...") and/or in your job accomplishments. A neat way that works in some circumstances is to provide a general job description first and then show key customers and projects.

What is the best way to describe my current and past positions?

There are two key ideas to consider.

First, start by explaining something about the company or organization you work for. Instead of just providing your employer's name, include at least a one-line description of what the firm or agency does. At some level, you can ride on the coattails of your employer. Including the fact that your employer is an "industry-leading provider of..." or "serves over 10,000 clients..." will enhance your personal role.

Next, be sure to provide some idea of the scope and responsibilities of each position. Although accomplishments are very important, it is still important to answer the question, "What do I do?" This section should follow the list of KEYWORDs you hopefully developed during your analysis of the job announcement. You do not have to use ALL of the KEYWORDs for each position, but collectively in your resume, you need to address all of them.

Include numbers. If you managed an IT budget, for example, say so and provide the amount. The same applies to any projects that you describe.

How do I select and then properly describe my accomplishments?

First of all, realize that your accomplishments do not all have to be worthy of the Nobel Prize. What the recruiter and hiring manager are looking for are just solid, specific examples in your work history that demonstrate that you really did what your resume describes. For example, if one of your KEYWORDs is SOFTWARE DEVELOPMENT, which provides a generic description of the design, development, and coding work that you performed, then in your Accomplishments section, you really should include a few actual examples of applications that you developed, with the specifics, including any numbers that are appropriate—the name of the application, what function it provided, the length of the code, the version number, the number of projected users, and the year or years you worked on this. To build your list of accomplishment, consider each KEYWORD and then try to come up with a specific example of when you did that.

Once you have a good list of accomplishments, be sure to give each accomplishment a title, and each product a name. If the project never really had a formal name, make one up that seems appropriate. For example, instead of just saying that you implemented a tracking system for all system changes, at least call it a System Change Log (capitalized). Instead of just saying that you implemented a process to deploy system patches, call it an Enterprise Patch Management System. This gives the impression that you developed something of lasting importance (which you probably did).

Should I include all of my IT training courses?

That depends on how long you have been in the workforce and how many training courses you have. If you are new to the IT workforce and have only a few training courses, include every one! If you have been around for a while and have lots and lots of training courses, include only those in the last 5-6 years and pick out of those the ones that are the most impressive and most applicable to the job you are applying for. If there is a certain course you know they are looking for, include it regardless of how long ago it was.

How many courses should I include?

Never more than 10 to 15. Adjust as needed for the final length of the resume.

Do I have to write a new resume for each position I apply to?

Yes and no. You truly do need to do a thorough KEYWORD analysis of each vacancy announcement you consider. If you really want to be rated as Best Qualified, it is very important to align your resume with the KEYWORDS you developed. Hopefully, if the position aligns well with your experience, you should be able to easily reorganize the information you already have in the job roles descriptions in your resume, around a slightly different set of KEYWORDs. You should also look carefully at the terminology in the announcement. If the announcement uses specific terms like "accountability" or "quantitative analysis" and your resume never uses these terms, you need to address this. Be careful NOT to just pull in long phrases from the announcement—recruiters are looking for your experience, not just a parroting of their announcement. However, the terminology you use should still ring true to their ears. If you find that the reworking is extreme, reconsider whether you are truly qualified for this position.

Can I use KEYWORDS in addition to the list I developed in my analysis?

Absolutely! No one's experience will exactly mirror the job announcement, plus the hiring manager may see an added value in some additional expertise that you bring! Assign appropriate KEYWORDs as needed to reflect your individual job experience. Just be sure to address each of the job roles you identified in the announcement at some point in your resume.

Do I have to spell out really common IT terms?

Yes. Even spell out Information Technology (IT) the first time you use it. Never assume that your reader understands any acronym. Beyond this, it is critically important that you start by explaining any system or project in a clear, simple fashion that any reasonably informed reader could understand. Even if the target hiring manager is an expert, he or she will be impressed that you understand the technology well enough to explain it to a lay reader.

What do I do if my job is classified?

First and foremost, follow the classification guidelines provided by the institution or agency that you serve. Remember that the hiring agency is not as interested in the specifics as it is in the key skills and experiences you have developed. It is perfectly acceptable, and mandatory, to show the name of your organization as CLASSIFIED and then only to provide an approved, generalized, high-level description of your job duties. Coupled with your security classification, this will be interpreted as an asset.

Focusing on Your IT Career

Remember that there is no substitute for experience and qualifications. Although an effective IT resume is a great tool to assist you in getting the positions and career to which you aspire, hiring managers inside and outside the government ultimately are looking for well-qualified and experienced employees. Consider that carefully as you evaluate and pursue both academic training and job opportunities. Getting a firm grounding in your field is paramount, and nothing will make you stand out more than good, solid experience in the key functions of your trade. Beyond that, a formal education is the best bet for future promotion potential. To get to senior positions inside or outside Information Technology, nothing beats a college education.

IT Customer Services, People Skills, and Other Soft Skills in Addition to Technical Skills

Many vacancy announcements will require both technical skills and soft skills that focus on customer service, advising management, user support, leading teams, and user software training. These people skills are critical regardless of grade level and specialization you are seeking.

Specialized Experience and KSAs

Almost all USAJOBS vacancy announcements will mention that candidates must possess at least one year of Specialized Experience at or equivalent to the next lower grade in the federal service in order to qualify for the position.

Specialized Experience is experience that is directly related to the position and has equipped the applicant with the particular knowledge, skills, and abilities (KSAs) to successfully perform the duties of the position, to include experience in applying and interpreting IT theories, principles, concepts, practices, knowledge management, and customer service support to IT clients. You should include the details under Specialized Experience and any KSA descriptions in your initial KEYWORD analysis; if you do this, your resume should clearly address each element described.

One of the key considerations often is how to address the KSAs. Candidates used to have to specifically address each KSA in a written narrative; however, that requirement has now been discouraged by the Federal-Wide Hiring Reform Initiative of 2010. You will have to read the vacancy announcement very carefully to determine how to address the KSAs. If the announcement stresses a very specific set of KSAs, it might be wise to include paragraph-length narratives within your resume to address each KSA. These could be included in either the job description or accomplishment sections and should be clearly marked as to which KSA they illustrate.

Required Core Competencies

USAJOBS vacancy announcements almost always also require IT specialists to address the set of 4 Core Competencies in addition to their technical skills. These competencies include Attention to Detail, Customer Service, Oral Communication, and Problem Solving, and assure the hiring agency that you have the experience and skill sets needed to be effective on the job, to be able to work with a broad range of people, and to be able to solve the problems that inevitably arise in any work environment. These core competencies are important for every IT specialist position. Be sure to cover these in your project or duties descriptions.

Attention to Detail

Is thorough when performing work and conscientious about attending to detail.

Customer Service

Works with clients and customers (that is, any individuals who use or receive the services or products that your work unit produces, including the general public, individuals who work in the agency, other agencies, or organizations outside the government) to assess their needs, provide information or assistance, resolve their problems, or satisfy their expectations; knows about available products and services; is committed to providing quality products and services.

Oral Communication

Expresses information (for example, ideas or facts) to individuals or groups effectively, taking into account the audience and nature of the information (for example, technical, sensitive, controversial); makes clear and convincing oral presentations; listens to others, attends to nonverbal cues, and responds appropriately.

Problem Solving

Identifies problems; determines accuracy and relevance of information; uses sound judgment to generate and evaluate alternatives, and to make recommendations.

So how do you address these Core Competencies? There are several options, and you can adjust the approach to your specific experience and resume style.

❯ **Use Competencies as KEYWORDs:** Customer Service would clearly be a key role for many IT professionals, as well as Oral and Written Communications, so either of these competencies could easily be used as a KEYWORD in your resume. See a few examples below.

❯ **Include Competencies in the Job Role Descriptions:** You can also just mention (and CAPITALIZE) these competencies within the job role descriptions associated with other KEYWORDs. The following examples illustrate this approach:

> OPERATIONAL ANALYSIS: Apply an ATTENTION TO DETAIL in evaluating and analyzing the impact of proposed new systems and proposed changes to existing operational systems. Complete an Analysis of Alternatives in developing and recommending alternate technical solutions. Develop qualitative and quantitative measures of effectiveness to be applied to project objectives.
>
> NETWORK ADMINISTRATION: Manage all Local Area Network and Wide Area Network (LAN/WAN) components, including Cisco and Juniper routers, switches, and firewalls. Install, configure, upgrade, and maintain local network hardware/software components. Leverage PROBLEM SOLVING SKILLS to troubleshoot and resolve complex network communication outages and performance issues.

❯ **Highlight Competencies in the Accomplishments:** Another equally effective approach is to highlight each of these skills in your accomplishments. See below for some examples using this model.

> **Capability Maturity Model (CMM):** *(Problem Solving)* Project Lead for a team-based effort to implement CMM for the Enterprise Document Archive system, a Knowledge Management (KM) repository. Led the team through a detailed analysis effort to identify process improvements needed for CMM certification. Process improvements recommended and implemented for the software development procedures during this 6-month effort resulted in a 30% gain in efficiency (2014).
>
> **Web Proxy Migration:** *(Attention to Detail)* Planned and executed a 4-month project to reconfigure the agency's web proxy implementation to split the web environment into two separate dedicated network segments. Led the enterprise network engineering team through the development of a detailed project plan that included network configuration steps, testing, phased implementation schedule, and rollback procedures. Completed the final phase of the migration in June 2015, with no impact to the operational environment (2015).

Top Ten List of **Accomplishments and Projects**

Developing (and maintaining) a list of your top accomplishments really makes it easy to develop or update your resume when you suddenly see that perfect job on USAJOBS. Coming up with a list of accomplishments in the IT field is really no different from any other field, except that it might even be easier to include lots of pertinent numbers, as you will often be able to include statistics like the number of systems, the number of impacted users, the version number of the software, and even the percentage of improvement in ticket closure rates, network latency, or system availability.

Here is a good method to develop an IT-related accomplishment. Let's say that you are applying for a software design and development position, so you obviously need to include examples of software products that you developed or at least updated.

Your first thought: Yes, I designed and developed a database application to make it easier to track the Requests for Change (RFCs) for our customer's organization.

Now gather some information on this achievement by asking yourself all the pertinent questions.

What was the name of the database?
It really didn't have one, but we could call it the RFC Tracking Database.

What was its purpose?
To track RFCs for our organization so we could keep track of the history, plus be able to track each RFC to its resolution and closure.

How did you get this task?
I actually suggested it after it became harder and harder to figure out whatever happened to each RFC.

What database and/or software was used? Microsoft Access

What version? Version 10

How long did it take you? About 3 months.

Did you do it all yourself?
Yes, but I did develop and vet the requirements through our Change Control Board.

Did you get an award for this effort?
No, but our customer wrote a nice compliment to my supervisor.

When did you complete this? June 2014

Now, you have all the details needed to develop a concise, but information-packed accomplishment:

> **RFC Tracking Database:** Developed and designed an RFC Tracking Database using Microsoft Access Version 10 to track Requests for Change (RFCs) for the customer organization, from initiation and presentation to the Change Control Board (CCB) through resolution and closure. Vetted requirements with the CCB and implemented the resulting product within a 3-month period. Received a written acknowledgement from the customer noting the significant improvement in RFC accountability (2014).

Here are some IT-related examples of potential accomplishments. Remember, developing and then maintaining a list of your personal accomplishments as your career evolves will make it a cinch to when it comes time to apply for a new position.

- Installing or upgrading to a new version of an operating system or layered application.
- Researching, testing, and recommending the application of a new technology.
- Completing a major network reconfiguration.
- Developing a Standard Operating Procedure (SOP).
- Designing and/or delivering a user training class.
- Representing your organization on an IT-related working group or board.
- Being selected to participate in a special study or to attend a technical conference.
- Managing or resolving a major system outage or performance issue.
- Recommending and implementing any business process changes that reduced the time to respond to system or network outages, or improved the user experience.
- Developing and delivering a technical presentation.
- Developing an IT-related Statement of Work (SOW) and/or assisting with the acquisition of IT systems or services.
- Analyzing an IT policy or regulation and its implications for your organization.
- Leading the Certification & Accreditation of an IT system.
- Resolving information security findings.
- Designing and implementing Active Directory policies.
- Managing a Technology Refresh effort—ordering, building, configuring, and training users on a new desktop platform.
- Designing and implementing a new technology or system configuration.
- Developing a major program plan such as a Configuration Management Plan, Acquisition Logistics Management Plan (ALSP), or System Security Management Plan.
- Developing a System Security Plan (SSP).
- Managing multiple software releases for a product (Release Management).
- Managing the application of security and other software patches.
- Managing the full Software Development Life Cycle (SDLC) for a software product (requirements traceability, developing, testing, transition to operations, and so on).
- Developing a website.

Michael Cedar
1000 Brooklane Street, Fairfax, VA 22031
Email: cedar123@mail.com
Phone: (321) 456-7890
Citizenship: U.S. Citizen | Veteran's Preference: N/A | Security Clearance: Secret

---

PROFILE

Certified Senior Information Security Services Specialist with hands-on expertise with advanced Cyber Security toolsets and processes that ensure the confidentiality, integrity, and availability of Agency information assets. Possess knowledge of Certification & Accreditation (C&A), Intrusion Detection, Vulnerability Assessment, Security Event Response, and Risk Management in the design of information security requirements, plans, and strategies needed to safeguard highly sensitive systems, data, and communications resources. Self-motivated and goal-oriented, with a demonstrated ability to handle complex responsibilities in a demanding work environment.

CERTIFICATIONS

Cisco Certified Entry Networking Technician (CCENT), 2015
Global Information Assurance Certification (GIAC) Certified Incident Handler (GCIH), 2014
Certified Ethical Hacker (CEH), 2014
Linux Server Professional Certification (LPIC-1), 2014
Certified Information Systems Security Professional (CISSP), 2012
GIAC Security Essentials Certification (GSEC), 2008

COMPUTER SKILLS

Cyber Security: Host Based Security System (HBSS), Websense Web Security Gateway, Nessus, AppDetective, WebInspect, Core Impact, Core InSight, nCircle, Symantec Data Loss Protection (DLP), Nitro Security Information and Event Management (SIEM), Bit9, Maas360, NetIQ, McAfee e-Policy Orchestrator (ePO), Qualys, WebScarab, Open Web Application Security Project (OWASP), Zed Attack Proxy (ZAP), Assured Compliance Assessment Solution (ACAS), Tripwire, Nmap (Network Mapper), Wireshark

Intrusion Detection: Sourcefire

Digital Forensics: Helix3, EnCase, Forensic Toolkit Imager (FTK Imager)

Database: MySQL, Microsoft SQL

Data Analysis: LogLogic

Network Inventory: Alloy Navigator, Alloy Discovery

Platforms: Linux (Redhat, CentOS, Ubuntu), Solaris, Windows Desktop XP/7/8, Windows Server 2K3/2K8/2K12

Network: Cisco routers/switches/ASAs

Scripting Tools: PHP, BASH, SED/AWK

Protocols: VPN, VLAN, DNS, DHCP, PPP, SMTP, IIS, ssh, Sendmail/Postfix, RAS, NAT, Sendmail, TCP/IP, VPN

Office Products/Groupware: Microsoft Office

EDUCATION

- MS, Information Security & Assurance, Ohio State University, Columbus, OH (2013)
- BS, Information Technology, University of Michigan, Ann Arbor, MI (2007)

RELATED PROFESSIONAL EXPERIENCE

IT Specialist (INFOSEC) (NT04) (08/2012 – Present)
Information Assurance Division, Department of Homeland Security
Washington, DC
Full-Time: 40+ hours/week
Base Salary: $99,296

VULNERABILITY ASSESSMENT: Serve as a technical resource to the Vulnerability Scanning Team. Develop custom audit files for file content scanning and provide technical assistance with the analysis and interpretation of scanning data collected by a Nessus-based vulnerability scanner. Provide expert assistance with the development, implementation, and maintenance of custom scripts and other automated tools required to scan Linux systems. Research and recommend new vulnerability assessment strategies and tools.

SECURITY TECHNOLOGIES & TOOLS: Implement, configure, update, patch, troubleshoot, and maintain critical Information Security tools that promote the security of enterprise systems and applications. Manage Websense web proxy implementation to ensure a real time response to network-based threats. Provide technical assistance for the implementation and deployment of a range of security tools, including Symantec Endpoint Protection and Host Based Security System (HBSS). Research, evaluate, recommend, and implement IT security solutions.

INFORMATION SECURITY SERVICES: As a member of the Information Assurance Compliance Team, provide Information Security services across the DHS enterprise. Recognized as a Senior Information Security Services Specialist, providing Information Assurance functions ensuring the confidentiality, integrity, and availability of over 1250 servers and desktop systems in a highly diverse computing and networking environment.

SECURITY EVENT RESPONSE: Monitor and analyze web traffic from Websense to identify, respond, and report suspicious traffic and potential security breaches. Participate in the Security Event Response Working Group, which interfaces with commercial vendors to identify and recommend enhanced intrusion detection solutions.

SELECTED ACCOMPLISHMENTS
- **Websense Proxy Migration:** Planned and executed a project to reconfigure the Websense web proxy implementation to split the web environment into two separate dedicated network segments. Worked with other senior network engineers to develop a detailed plan including rollback steps. Successfully completed the migration in nonworking hours over one weekend, with no impact to operations.
- **IDS Consolidation Working Group:** Participant in the Intrusion Detection System (IDS) section of the IT Consolidation Working Group. Provide information security advice and recommendations during the process to achieve a more consolidated, centralized solution for intrusion detection across all joint-agency fusion centers.

Information Security Consultant (09/2009 – 08/2012)
Computer Technology Group
Santa Barbara, CA
Full-Time: 40+ hours/week
Base Salary: $93,558.40

SECURITY EVENT RESPONSE: Monitored, analyzed, and responded to local and widespread events generated by the Intrusion Detection System. Investigated and identified potential breaches in network, hardware, and software system configurations. Worked with Security Operations Center

(SOC) personnel to differentiate false positives from true intrusion attempts and reported all true positives to FAS management and to US-CERT, following US-CERT incident reporting guidelines.

INFORMATION SECURITY SERVICES: Oversaw security πadministration for systems and databases for the General Services Administration (GSA) Federal Acquisition Service (FAS), which provides solutions to Federal clients in the areas of technology, transportation, travel, motor vehicle management, products and services, and procurement. Supported systems and applications for over 40 application development groups across the FAS. This included Windows, Linux (CentOS and Redhat), and Solaris servers, as well as multiple database management systems.

SECURITY TECHNOLOGIES AND TOOLS: Maintained and updated information security tools and their underlying host systems. Utilized an advance tool set of commercial and open source products (Nessus, AppDetective, WebInspect, Core Impact, Core InSight, nCircle) to conduct technical security assessments of hosts, websites, and databases.

VULNERABILITY ASSESSMENT: Executed recurring, automated security scans of FAS production systems; coordinated system scanning schedules with the customer, and guided other information security personnel through the scanning process. Performed data analysis of technical security assessments to determine the security posture of IT assets. Validated vulnerabilities using Proof-of-Concept code and open source tools.

PATCH MANAGEMENT: Assessed system patch levels associated with all network and firewall requests. Enforced required software and security patch levels before granting system access to the network. Assessed patch management requirements for the Information Security systems and tools and applied required updates in compliance with FAS and US-CERT guidelines.

CUSTOMER SERVICE: Provided security engineering expertise to developers and management of the FAS application teams. Responded to network connectivity issues identified by internal business groups. Communicated complex and sensitive technical issues orally and in writing to technical and non-technical professionals to ensure awareness of Information Assurance compliance goals.

SELECTED ACCOMPLISHMENTS
- **Core InSight Deployment:** Task Lead for the implementation of the Core InSight web scanning appliance. Coordinated the hardware/software installation and configuration; designed and verified security credentials and firewall rules; and implemented automated scanning algorithms for all FAS-maintained websites.
- **Symantec Data Loss Prevention (DLP) Implementation:** Managed the full project life cycle to implement Symantec DLP for the FAS infrastructure. DLP is a data security product that discovers, monitors, and protects confidential data assets. Coordinated and evaluated a Proof of Concept implementation; planned and deployed an operational instance; configured file scans across all FAS servers; and implemented data analysis procedures.

GS-1102

Acquisition Professional

Contracting positions are a very specialized job classification in the federal government. Positions included in this series:

- ❯ Contract Specialist
- ❯ Contract Administrator
- ❯ Procurement Analyst

Those interested in entering this field must meet basic education requirements (GS-7, GS-9, GS-11) or meet basic education requirements and possess valid specialized experience (GS-12 and above) to qualify for positions in the GS-1102 classification series.

Basic Requirements for GS-5 through GS-12

- A 4-year course of study leading to a bachelor's degree with a major in any field; or

- At least 24 semester hours in any combination of the following fields: accounting, business, finance, law, contracts, purchasing, economics, industrial management, marketing, quantitative methods, or organization and management. Applicants who meet the criteria for Superior Academic Achievement qualify for positions at the GS-7 level.

Grade	Education	Specialized Experience
GS-7	1 full academic year of graduate education or law school or superior academic achievement	1 year equivalent to at least GS-5
GS-9	2 full academic years of progressively higher level graduate education or masters or equivalent graduate degree or LL.B. or J.D.	1 year equivalent to at least GS-7
GS-11	3 full academic years of progressively higher level graduate education or Ph.D. or equivalent doctoral degree	1 year equivalent to at least GS-9
GS-12 and above	No educational equivalent	1 year equivalent to at least the next lowest grade level

Source: https://www.opm.gov/policy-data-oversight/classification-qualifications/general-schedule-qualification-policies/#url=General-Policies

Basic Requirements for GS-13 and Above

- Completion of all mandatory training prescribed by the head of the agency for progression to GS-13 or higher level contracting positions, including at least 4-years experience in contracting or related positions. At least 1 year of that experience must have been specialized experience at or equivalent to work at the next lower level of the position, and must have provided the knowledge, skills, and abilities to perform successfully the work of the position. **AND**

- A 4-year course of study leading to a bachelor's degree, that included or was supplemented by at least 24 semester hours in any combination of the following fields: accounting, business, finance, law, contracts, purchasing, economics, industrial management, marketing, quantitative methods, or organization and management.

Qualifying **Experience**

What is qualifying specialized experience?

Soliciting, evaluating, negotiating, and awarding contracts with commercial organizations, educational institutions, nonprofit organizations, and State, local, or foreign governments for furnishing products, services, construction or research, and development. The full realm of experience also includes: contract administration, contract termination, analyzing and evaluation cost or price proposals, and contract closeout. This type of experience is qualifying when gained in the private sector, non-profit arena, in the military, and in the Federal Government (civilian and DoD agencies).

NOTE: It is important to read each job announcement carefully to identify specific experience requirements as well as competencies identified as evaluation factors in order to ensure your resume corroborates your answers given in the assessment questionnaire.

What is NOT considered qualifying specialized experience?

Activities associated with the use of the Government Purchase Card, or work as a Contracting Officer Representative or budget official.

Federal Acquisition Certification

The Federal Acquisition Certification in Contracting (FAC-C) Program is for contracting professionals in the Federal Government performing contracting and procurement activities and functions. The purpose of this program is to establish general education, training, and experience requirements for those contracting professionals. The FAC-C applies to all executive agencies, except the Department of Defense (DoD).

Find out information about the FAC-C Program on the Federal Acquisition Institute webiste at https://www.fai.gov/drupal/certification/contracting-fac-c.

Example of Qualifying Experience from Actual Resumes

Fed to Fed (GS-11 Contract Specialist to GS-12 Contract Specialist)

CONTRACT MANAGEMENT: Conduct cradle to grave contracting activities including pre- and post-award processes and procedures (acquisition planning, market research, solicitation/evaluation, negotiation, administration, award, and closeout); apply contract administration principles and practices including monitoring contractor performance, preparation of contract modifications and negotiation strategies, making recommendations for termination, and reviewing and approving expenditures prior to contract closeout. Participate in various teams to improve and streamline work processes; brainstorm alternative solutions to ongoing contractual problems, evaluate effectiveness of process change and revise accordingly for continuous improvement. Proficient in the execution of various contract functions in the ever changing federal acquisition environment. For example, ensure compliance with White House initiatives on improving federal contracting through increased contract administration, reduce spending, and reduce the use of high-risk contracting authorities such as noncompetitive contracting and labor-hour contracts that pose special risks of overspending.

ACQUISITION PLANNING: Actively participate in the planning process with major stakeholders to develop a sound business approach for acquiring goods and services in support of the Agency's mission. Collaborate with program officials; Contracting Officer Representatives (CORs); and other interested parties to ensure commitment to the plan throughout the acquisition process. Strive to promote full and open competition and develop the overall strategy for managing the acquisition in accordance with Federal Acquisition Regulation (FAR) Part 7. Assist and offer guidance to CORs on the development of performance work statements (PWS) and statements of work (SOWs). Assist managers, scientific personnel, and facilities engineers with defining acquisition needs and requirements to avoid ambiguities in the solicitation.

MARKET RESEARCH: Perform market research using a variety of sources including the Internet, supplier catalogs, existing user information, and GSA schedule vendors. Collect and analyze information from known sources for both specific products and services to compare quality, pricing, demographic availability, etc. Make recommendations/decisions based on research findings.

SOLICITATION AND EVALUATION: Develop and issue solicitation documents identifying the Agency's requirements to the vendor community and include solicitation provisions and contract clauses as prescribed in FAR Part 52, e.g., payments and funding; representations and certifications; information required when submitting a proposal; evaluation factors; etc. Review evaluation factors to ensure consistency with the SOW/PWS and also to ensure factors are clear and concise to avoid ambiguity and the need to issue amendments to the solicitation. Receive and evaluate business proposals; address initial meeting of the technical evaluation team to provide instructions, discuss conflict of interest, and provide assistance as needed. Review and analyze proprietary pricing information received from vendors; ensure the secure storage of confidential and sensitive acquisition data to avoid compromising the acquisition process; discuss and share sensitive information with only those involved in the acquisition. Obtain and analyze detailed information from CORs in the form of a technical evaluation of proposals submitted in response to a solicitation; review results presented in accordance with the technical evaluation criteria contained in the solicitation. Utilize both business and technical data to make contractual decisions/recommendations in accordance with applicable FAR regulations.

NEGOTIATION AND AWARD: Enter into discussions with numerous potential contractors; program officials; and other major stakeholders in the acquisition process concerning the terms and conditions of a particular requirement to ensure all parties understand roles and responsibilities; discuss legal compliance requirements, payment processes, delivery terms, and product specifications; and interpret complex FAR clauses—for instance, find alternatives to goods and services that cannot be delivered for one reason or another and negotiate an acceptable replacement and/or monetary consideration for delivery past the negotiated timeframe. Determine the need to renegotiate contracts in the event of a claim to address complex invoice issues. Use past performance information and debarment and suspension information to ensure potential contractors are responsible to perform and provide quality service to the federal government prior to entering into a contractual arrangement.

CONTRACT ADMINISTRATION: Perform contract administration and resolve problems independently on a variety of contracts including maintenance agreements with option years, janitorial services, professional services (research), and temporary staffing services. Administer complex professional scientific services contract in the area of hydrology research of approximately $2 million; administer $1.5 million janitorial contract shared between three facilities. Work closely with COR in monitoring contractor performance to ensure contractor is in compliance with legal requirements, FAR, and the terms and conditions of the contract, e.g., delivery schedules are met, products and services meet required standards, services are provided in accordance with SOW. Prepare contract modifications; facilitate contractor meetings, as necessary; maintain accurate and legally defensible contract documentation including original contract, all correspondence, changes/deviations, modifications, payment schedules, and performance reports. Diligently evaluate contractor performance and, as necessary, proceed with recommendations for suspension and debarment for those who behave unethically or engage in poor performance of government-funded work. Compile and analyze financial data during the contract closeout process to address outstanding invoices, claims, and other financial contract obligations such as the use of prior year and no-year funds in accordance with Payment Clauses in the FAR.

Military to Fed (Wing Staff Group Superintendent, U. S Air Force to GS-9 Contract Specialist)

(This applicant qualifies for a GS-9 based on education alone but also possesses some specialized experience in acquisition, providing the potential to qualify for a GS-11 Contract Specialist).

BUSINESS ACUMEN: Thorough understanding and knowledge of trends in Federal acquisition practices, current and future policies, and business strategy. Possess knowledge of the Defense Federal Acquisition Regulation (DFAR) and the Federal Acquisition Regulation (FAR) sufficient to understand, interpret, and apply in a variety of routine and complex acquisition situations. Demonstrated experience participating in a variety of contract types: Other than Full and Open Competition (FAR Subpart 6.3); Negotiation (FAR Part 15); Commercial Items (FAR Part 12); and Simplified Acquisitions (FAR Part 13).

CONTRACT MANAGEMENT: Participate in/conduct pre- and post-award processes and procedures (acquisition planning, market research, evaluation, negotiation, administration, and award); apply contract administration principles and practices including monitoring contractor performance, assisting with the preparation of contract modifications and negotiation strategies, making recommendations for termination, and reviewing and approving expenditures prior to contract closeout.

ACQUISITION PLANNING: Determine product/service need including price, quantity, quality, and specifications on a quarterly basis; provide information to budget officer/ senior officer to plan scheduled purchases in order to avoid work stoppage situations. Acquisition planning activities affect entire base and staff in the performance of mission-critical daily duties. For items over the micro-purchase threshold, develop contract requirements including specifications, delivery schedules, performance, etc. Market Research—Perform market research using a variety of sources including the

Internet, supplier catalogs, existing user information, and GSA schedule vendors. Collect and analyze information from known sources for both specific products and services to compare quality, pricing, demographic availability, etc. Make recommendations/decisions based on research findings.

Key Accomplishment:
Led effort for emergency acquisition of security door system to avert a major security violation. Electronic Security Door system became inoperable at Central Command and Control Center, creating an emergency state of vulnerability; classified information at risk. Assessed immediate needs of entire base; conducted pre-solicitation meeting with key personnel including vendors, civil engineers, contracting officials to discuss accelerated award schedule. Directed walk-through of area and conducted a question and answer session for attendees. Orally requested proposal submission within a week; received and evaluated proposals; secured funding obligation and other necessary approvals; and forwarded recommendations to contracting officer to execute award document. Results: Personally negotiated a fixed price contract, including delivery and installation schedules; training of base personnel on the system, and maintenance on equipment for 1 year. Ultimately avoided breach in security that could have placed lives in danger and led to mission failure.

What competencies (knowledge, skills, and abilities) must federal acquisition professionals possess to successfully perform the critical duties of their assigned positions? Contract Specialists are looked upon as business managers in the federal acquisition arena, which requires knowledge in both the technical and professional aspects of contracting.

There are 11 units of competence (10 technical units and 1 professional unit) covering the various phases of the acquisition process. The 10 technical units cover everything from pre-award activities to solicitation to proposal evaluation, negotiation, award, administration, and closeout. The professional unit covers what are commonly referred to as "soft skills"—skills such as problem solving, customer service, oral and written communications, and interpersonal skills, to name a few. Soft skills alone are not enough to qualify you for a position in the field of acquisition, but rather a combination of both technical and professional skills as outlined in each individual vacancy announcement.

Refer to the competency chart on the Department of Defense (DOD) Defense Procurement and Acquisition Policy (DPAP) website listed below which provides the reader with a comprehensive breakdown of the core competencies and the specific elements of each competency.

Pre-Award and Award

Develop and/or Negotiate Positions

Advanced Cost and/or Price Analysis

Contract Administration

Small Business/Socio-Economic Programs

Negotiate FPRAs & Administer Cost Accounting Standards

Contract Termination

Procurement Policy

Other Competencies

Contracting in a Continengent and/or Combat Environment

Problem Solving

Customer Service

Oral Communication

Written Communication

Interpersonal Skills

Decisiveness

Technical Credibility

Flexibility

Resilience

Accountability

DPAP webpage on Contracting Competencies:
http://www.acq.osd.mil/dpap/ops/contracting_competency_assessment.html

Link to download the Contracting Competency Model:
http://www.acq.osd.mil/dpap/ops/docs/cca-contractingcompetencymodel.xls

Qualifying Experience

Following is a segment from the chart to give you an idea of what is expected from an acquisition professional in the federal government:

Pre-Award and Award	Determination of How Best to Satisfy Requirements for the Mission Area	1. Provide proactive business advice on requirements documentation based on analysis of requirements and performance-based approaches to find the best solution to satisfy mission requirements.
		2. Conduct market research using relevant resources prior to solicitation to understand the industry environment and determine availability of sources of supply and/or services.
		3. Perform acquisition planning by considering all available sources and methods of procurement to satisfy mission needs while appropriately allocating risk.
	Consider Socio-economic Requirements	4. Consider socio-economic requirements including small business, labor, environmental, foreign, and other socio-economic requirements to provide maximum practicable contracting and subcontracting opportunities.
	Promote Competition	5. Conduct pre-solicitation industry conferences and analyze responses to draft solicitation terms and conditions to promote full and open competition.
		6. Identify and facilitate joint ventures and partnering on solicitations and subcontracting opportunities to increase competition and/or small business participation.
	Source Selection Planning	7. Document a source selection plan that is consistent with public law, regulations, policy, and other guidelines.
	Solicitation of Offers	8. Conduct pre-bid or pre-proposal conference to inform offerors of the requirements of the acquisition.
		9. Publicize proposed procurements to promote competition.
		10. Issue a written solicitation consistent with the requirements documents, acquisition plan and source selection plan, that includes the appropriate provisions and clauses tailored to the requirement.
		11. Issue amendments or cancel solicitations when such actions are in the best interest of the Government and conform to law and regulations.
		12. Respond to preaward inquiries by taking the appropriate action according to FAR/DFARS (and applicable supplements) to resolve questions.
	Responsibility Determination	13. Determine contractor responsibility by assessing past performance and financial stability to ensure that the contractor will be able to satisfy Government requirements.
	Bid Evaluation (Sealed Bidding)	14. Evaluate the sealed bids in an transparent manner to preserve the integrity of the competitive
		15. Perform price analysis to determine whether the lowest evaluated bid is reasonable and provides the best value to the Government.
	Proposal Evaluation (Contracting by Negotiation)	16. Evaluate proposals and quotes against evaluation criteria and request technical and pricing support, if needed, to identify offers that are acceptable or can be made acceptable.
	Source Selection	17. Decide whether to hold discussions based on results of the evaluation.
		18. Establish the competitive range to determine which of the offers will not be considered for the award.
	Contract Award	19. Select the awardee who in the Government's estimation, provides the best value.
		20. Award contract/ Issue task or delivery orders after ensuring fund availability and obtaining reviews and approvals.
		21. Conducting pre/post award debriefings for all unsuccessful offerors when requested to ensure appropriate disclosure of information.
	Process Protests	22. Process protests to determine whether to withhold award or stop performance pending outcome of the protest.
Develop and/or Negotiate Positions	Justification of Other than Full and Open	23. Justify the need to negotiate or award the contract without full and open competition or, in a multiple award scenario, without providing for fair opportunity based on business strategies and market research.
	Terms and Conditions	24. Determine terms and conditions, including special contract requirements applicable to the acquisition, that are appropriate for the acquisition to comply with laws and regulations (e.g. method of financing, Government property, intellectual property, OCI, specialty metals).
	Preparation and Negotiation	25. Prepare for negotiations / discussions / awards by reviewing audit and technical reports, performing cost and/or price analysis (or reviewing price analysts reports), and developing pre-negotiation position to include identifying potential trade-offs.
		26. Negotiate terms and conditions (including price) based on the pre-negotiation objective and give-and-take with the offeror to establish a fair and reasonable price.

The chart above is an excerpt from the Contracting Competency Model link found at http://www.acq.osd.mil/dpap/ops/contracting_competency_assessment.html.

DEBORAH S. SMITH

1111 Manassas Way
Manassas, VA 22009
Daytime Phone: (300) 888-8888   Evening Phone: (200) 777-7777
E-mail: Deborah.smith@gmail.com

PROFESSIONAL EXPERIENCE

CONTRACT SPECIALIST (GS-1102-11)   09/2008–Present
Eastern Branch Service Center/Acquisition Branch   40 hours/week
Agricultural Research Services (ARS) U.S. Department of Agriculture (USDA)
Acting Branch Chief: Richard Budd, (999) 999-9999, may contact

MANAGE THE FULL RANGE OF CONTRACT FUNCTIONS as a Level 1 warranted Contracting Officer (COR) for the ARS and other USDA agencies. Administer all phases of the acquisition lifecycle from pre-award to post-award and close-out, including price analysis, price negotiations, performance monitoring, and contract administration.

REVIEW, ANALYZE, PROCESS AND MANAGE VARIOUS CONTRACT TYPES to procure services and supplies including IT licensing software and equipment. Plan and execute pre/post-award procurement actions using a range of contract methods and types i.e., firm-fixed price (FFP), Blank Purchase Agreements (BPAs), indefinite delivery/indefinite quantity (IDIQ), and non-standard terms and conditions to include fixed-price, incentives, and escalation provisions. Support development complex, competitive solicitations. Conduct market research, price analysis, monitor contract performance, and review proposals.

ACQUISITION PLANNING: Develop Government Cost Estimates (IGCE) during acquisition planning. Assist and offer guidance with the development of performance work statements (PWS), specification documents and performance requirements. Assist managers, scientific personnel and facilities engineers with defining acquisition needs, requirements and locating sources. Develop effective and realistic acquisition plans in coordination with customer needs.

FEDERAL ACQUSITION LAWS, regulations, policies, and procedures to ensure all goods and services are procured in compliance with Federal Acquisition Regulations (FAR) and AGAR (the agency supplemental). Lead contract negotiations. Monitor contract performance and negotiate modifications to ensure satisfactory progress, completion of activities, and compliance with terms and conditions. Ensure milestones are met. Assist program office with rewriting the Statement of Work if needed.

RESEARCH, ANALYSIS & DOCUMENTATION: Review acquisition packages for completeness and sufficient funding. Research and analyze procurement sources. Resolve contractual issues. Develop and complete procurement documents, including Contract Action Reports (CARs). Make recommendations for managers following contract reviews. Issue accurate and timely amendments to solicitations (as needed) and contract modifications. Establish and maintain close-out files in accordance with established deadlines.

USE RANGE OF SYSTEMS AND SOFTWARE including the Integrated Acquisition System (IAS), Federal Financial System (FFS), Acquisition Tracking System (ATS), and Microsoft Access, Word and Excel to track funding. Input CARs in the Federal Procurement Data System. Provide assistance to others with ATS and IAS issues. Prepare FedBizOpps and other posting announcements such as GSA e-Buy.

KEY CONTRACTS NEGOTIATED AND MANAGED

- Administered over 20 contracts, including maintenance agreements with option years, janitorial, professional services (research), temporary staffing services, and ground maintenance services for the US Arboretum.
- Administer complex professional scientific services contract in the area of hydrology research of about $2 million.
- Administer $1.5 million janitorial contract being shared between three facilities, including the US National Arboretum.
- Perform simplified purchases up to $150K for supplies and services such as lab equipment, furniture, and temp services.
- Award simplified contracts up to $150K and GSA schedule up to $1 million.

- In light of multiple staff turnover during FY2013, numerous contracts and purchase orders were reassigned to me (in addition to the already-assigned workload) with incomplete or no documentation and multiple issues. To effectively correct the situation, I reconstructed files, issued modifications, and **completed all actions slated for award during fiscal year (FY) 2013.**

- In addition to completing COR duties this past FY, assisted other staff members with a variety of issues, including issuance of notices in Federal Business Opportunities (FBO), technical assistance with the ATS and IAS, critical file reorganization, and human resource advisement.

TECHNOLOGY TRANSFER TECHNICAL ASSISTANT (GS-303-08)   10/2002–09/2008
Office of Technology, Transfer and Development (OTTAD)   40 hours/week
National Heart, Lung, & Blood Institute, NIH
Former Supervisor: Ms. Lillian Skyler, (301) 333-3333, may contact

DATABASE AND RECORDKEEPING SYSTEM: Classified, indexed, entered, and tracked all data in Knowledge Sharing System (KSS) TechTracs, a client/service and web-based system that provides intellectual asset management for over 400 Technology Transfer Agreements (TTAs). Entered TTA data in the KSS TechTracs automated system for the National Heart, Lung, & Blood Institute (NHLBI) and six NIH service centers.

MONITORED AND TRACKED EXPENSES for NHLBI and the six service centers. Reviewed expense summary reports generated by the Administrative Office. Prepared and submitted purchase orders for office supplies, training, travel and other expenditures.

ROYALTY ADMINISTRATION: Maintained royalty information, communications, and files. Drafted royalty letters and provide semi-annual statements. Formulated and distributed quarterly statements to current and former NHLBI inventors. Reviewed NIH Patent Licensing Activities reports. Responded to and resolved royalty inquiries. Assisted in rectifying inconsistencies in royalty agreements.

Key Accomplishments:
- Revamped an inconsistent and unreliable electronic filing system. Developed and implemented an improved coding system, which has provided more accurate and reliable data access and improved organization of over 400 technology transfer agreements. Corrected numerous inaccuracies in paper and electronic file classifications. Meticulously entered new data in the system, to ensure specialists can retrieve, amend, and generate reports.

EDUCATION

Master of Business Administration, May 2005, <u>Trinity Washington University</u>, Washington, DC
Total credits: 45 semester credits; Cumulative GPA: 3.713 Relevant Course Work: Economics, Strategic Management, Public Finance, Communications, Qualitative Methods, and Statistics.

Bachelor of Arts in Business Administration, May 1998, <u>Trinity Washington University</u>, Washington, D.C., Total credits: 135 semester credits

PROFESSIONAL TRAINING

- Project Management: Skills for Success, Learning Tree International (four-day course)
- FAC-C Level 1 courses, completed and certified (2012)
- FAC-C Level 2 courses completed: CON 214, CON 215, CON 216, and CON 217
- Level 1 Warranted Contracting Officer

HONORS & AWARDS

- Certificate of Appreciation from the USDA/OCIO Cyber Security Branch for the professional guidance and assistance provided at fiscal year-end, 2010
- Received numerous performance, special act, and time off awards as well as a special recognition plaque from the Director of NHLBI for exemplary service while employed at NIH.

GS-0343

Management and Program Analyst

The Management and Program Analyst position is the least well known to private-industry applicants and possibly the most prevalent management position in government. Many current federal employees strive to move into the Management Analyst occupational series so that they can be promoted to higher grade levels, work on projects that will improve and enhance government services to the American public, and have diverse and challenging work. You will see in this chapter that the Management Analyst positions are all different, and you will need to read each vacancy announcement to determine whether you are qualified for a particular position. Some positions are very technical, requiring subject-matter knowledge; others are general and require basic skills in program or management analysis, writing, and oral communications skills.

Note: Management Analysts are also often known as Project Managers.

According to Ligaya J. Fernandez, Senior Research Analyst for the Office of Policy and Evaluation at the U.S. Merit Systems Protection Board:

The Management and Program Analyst positions are very important in government... yes, these positions are critical in government. The government does not provide products to the public. The government provides services. These services are based on programs that government policymakers have determined the American public needs and wants, and so they pass laws to make sure that these services are provided to the people. Once the laws are passed, the executive branch of government implements them. Management and Program Analysts are involved in the process of passing and implementing the laws...they actually do the analytical work required, from which important decisions are made.

Decisions are based on information. Information (or data) has to be gathered, organized, and analyzed. And Management and Program Analysts do the gathering, the organizing, and the analyzing of information so that decisions can be made. Many are involved in program funding; and so many Program Analyst jobs require an understanding of financial management.

Once a law is passed and implemented, the government also needs to know if the program is working the way Congress said it should work. They need to know if the program is cost-effective or if improvements are needed. Answers to these and other questions are very important to the policymakers. And the people who are assigned the task of answering questions like these are the Management and Program Analysts. They gather essential information, organize and study it, analyze it, and then make recommendations to government officials by way of formal reports.

The requirements for, and responsibilities of, a Management and Program Analyst differ from job to job depending on grade, organization, location, etc. Reading the vacancy announcement very carefully is key to understanding what the job is all about. Some will require specialized subject-matter knowledge; but generally, they don't. What is required is knowledge and skill that would enable them to perform analytical and evaluative work regarding the agency's operation or management of its programs.

The basic qualification needed for these types of jobs is the knowledge of the theories, function, and processes of management so that analysts can identify problems and recommend solutions. (And so, there really is no specific education required for these jobs, although coursework that includes math, statistics, economics, accounting, and finance is very helpful.) These types of jobs also require knowledge of the different analytical tools and evaluative techniques needed to analyze qualitative and quantitative data.

In sum...I would say the importance of this series is this: Important government program decisions are made based on what Management and Program Analysts recommend, so candidates for these jobs better be good!

Management Analyst **Job Announcements**

Here are two excerpts from Management Analyst announcements. Each position is similar in terms of skills, but the area of specialization is different—Immigration/International Securities and Veterans Health Administration. Each federal agency will hire Management Analysts to analyze, evaluate, and give recommendations for change and improvement for their agency or office programs.

**Program & Management Analyst Position—Immigration, Headquarters' Intra-Agency Coordination & Protocol Division
U.S. Citizenship and Immigration Services, Department of Homeland Security, GS-0343-13/14**

U.S. Citizenship and Immigration Services secures America's promise as a nation of immigrants by providing accurate and useful information to our customers, granting immigration and citizenship benefits, promoting an awareness and understanding of citizenship, and ensuring the integrity of our immigration system.

Every day, the Management and Program Analysts:
* Implement, coordinate, and/or analyze a variety of management programs.
* Prepare and/or provide briefings and presentations.
* Develop and/or evaluate policies.

As Management and Program Analyst in the Headquarters' Intra-Agency Coordination & Protocol Division, your duties and responsibilities will include:
* Developing guidance and processes for USCIS-wide engagement with external stakeholders.
* Managing and tracking engagement conducted by the agency using applicable tools and resources.
* Supporting the planning and execution of all high-profile events and public USCIS initiatives.
* Developing written guidance and processes for defining internal communication and coordination protocols within the agency.
* Developing processes for implementation of an effective feedback loop.
* Coordinating and tracking agency participation in national, regional, and international events and working closely with the DHS Speaker's Bureau.
* Leading in planning and executing high-profile events and public USCIS initiatives.

Program & Management Analyst Position—Veterans Health Administration, National Office of Compliance
Dept. of Veterans Affairs, Veterans Health Administration, GS-0343-11/12

This position is located within the National Office of Compliance within the Office of Patient Care Services of VA Medical Centers in various locations throughout the United States. The National Office of Compliance is a new transformational program whose primary purpose is to assist medical centers in aligning their processes and practices with regulations and standards. This assistance will provide on-site assessment, consultation, education, and action plan development. The National Office of Compliance will work synergistically with all VHA departments including the Office of Nursing Service, Infection Control, Logistics, Systems Redesign, Quality Management, Patient Safety, and others.

Program Analysts provide oversight and education of administrative policies, programs, and operations for the Regional and National Office of Compliance and its affiliates with regard to the integration and adherence to Program and Process Compliance. Duties include, but are not limited to, the following:

- Handle issues related to program assessment and prepare communication to all levels of the healthcare system;
- Act as a liaison regarding communication with persons and groups within and outside the Regional and National Office of Compliance;
- Analyze and evaluate designs, studies, proposals, ideas, and best practices submitted by field facilities;
- Work with an interdisciplinary, structured performance improvement model to ensure customers and stakeholders are satisfied in a high-quality, cost-efficient, and schedule-compliant manner;
- Collaborate with team members in the study of system interactions and relations to people, information, equipment, and material to predict the best results to be obtained;
- Collaborate with and support the Regional and National Office of Compliance and facilitate Strategic Planning, Performance Measures, and Utilization Management Programs with emphasis on Access, Value, Efficiency, and Performance Improvement goals;
- Identify and develop action plans and work with educational and redesign specialists to develop and implement training programs for a diverse group of employees;
- Collect data and coordinate reports, projects, and initiatives related to customer service and access.

Key Skill: Qualitative and Quantitative Analysis

Many jobseekers will find this terminology in vacancy announcements. A recent workshop attendee at the Drug Enforcement Administration asked me in a course, "What does an announcement mean when they ask for experience in qualitative and quantitative methods?" This is a good question. I see this in many announcements. Think about when you measure qualitative and qualitative numbers about a program, budget, or office performance.

Knowledge of qualitative and quantitative methods for analyzing workload trends and survey data; assessing and improving complex management processes and systems, and program effectiveness.

A Management Analyst designs and conducts quantitative and qualitative analyses to evaluate and report on cost/benefit matters, financial issues, and organizational performance. The differences in qualitative and quantitative analyses are in the way data or information is collected in conducting a study. Simply stated, it is a difference between the use of numbers and words when conducting a study or evaluation. Quantitative analysis involves the utilization of questionnaires, tests, and existing databases. Qualitative analysis employs observations, interviews, and focus groups.

Collecting information using quantitative techniques is typically used to evaluate obvious behavior, and this methodology permits comparison and replication. And in most instances, it is believed that the reliability and validity of a study may be determined more objectively than when using quantitative techniques.

Utilizing qualitative methodologies to conduct an evaluation permits the consideration of concepts that were not part of the predetermined subject areas. Therefore, using qualitative techniques in conducting a study can be more exploratory in nature.

In summary, if you are applying for any kind of analyst or technician position, it would be very good to mention the types of qualitative and quantitative skills you have and the types of information you have analyzed.

Career Change with Management Analyst Positions

The Management Analyst series is an excellent choice for career development. Because these positions vary among agencies and offices, you can write your current resume featuring your projects and skills that are similar to what is described in this chapter. Changing careers to a Management Analyst position will involve analyzing the top skills needed in the target position and highlighting those same skills in your job.

Transitioning from Specific Positions

Here are some tips for transitioning from specific positions:

- If you are currently an Administrative Assistant, write about your special projects, database development, research, problem solving, setting up more efficient systems, and giving recommendations to the supervisor to improve operations.

- If you are currently a Lead Accounting Technician, GS-8, and hope to change series and move up a grade, you emphasize your problem solving, special projects, research and analysis, consulting, and advising customers about efficient methods of accounting information management and reports, including spreadsheets.

- If you are currently a Housing Management Specialist, GS-12, and would like to move into the Management Analyst series at a GS-12 or GS-13 level, you would want to emphasize your projects, partnerships with agencies, consulting services to housing entities, problem solving, analysis of programs, skills in spreadsheet design, and briefings written and given on housing topics. The focus of the project is on the analytical skills, not the content of housing.

Changing Levels

Changing careers at the GS-9 or GS-11 level is easier than at the higher grade levels because the qualifications for the positions usually are more general, such as this one:

> One year of specialized experience that equipped the applicant with the particular knowledge, skills, and abilities to perform successfully the duties of the position, and that is typically in or related to the work of the position to be filled. This experience must be equivalent to the GS-9 level in the federal government. Examples of such experience may include: analyzing the effectiveness of programs; analyzing the efficiency of operations; participating in studies to increase efficiency; preparing work plans and reports based on existing procedures or observations of activities; preparing materials for workflow and operational analyses, studies of costs, or equipment utilization; reviewing operational plans and current and incoming work projects; making recommendations for improving work methods; advising on the adequacy of budgets; and determining the need for work standards and control systems.

Project **Map**

Most Program and Management Analysts in government manage multiple projects in their jobs. The best way to write an impressive Management Analyst federal resume is to write about the projects you have managed. You can follow the Project Map in the graphic below to create a project list that addresses the following six critical skills for a Management Analyst. Use specific examples to prove your competencies and add them to your federal resume. In USAJOBS, you can also include your project list in the Additional Information section.

Add your projects for each knowledge, skill, or ability in the map below.

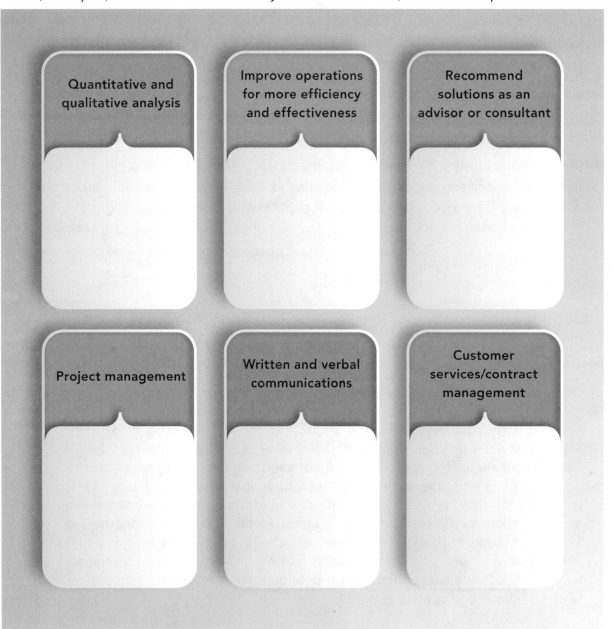

Quantitative and qualitative analysis

Improve operations for more efficiency and effectiveness

Recommend solutions as an advisor or consultant

Project management

Written and verbal communications

Customer services/contract management

Use Accomplishments to **Prove Your Top Level Skills**

Expand your project map into narrative descriptions of your projects and analytical tasks. Define your projects and accomplishments with quantifiable numbers for excellent, impressive, on-target content for your resume. The projects or stories will be useful for interview preparation as well because most federal interviews are behavior-based and require specific examples or stories as answers.

Here is a highly effective project outline that you can use to build your project list:

Accomplishment title:

Your role, name of task, project description, and date:

Budget (if applicable):

Challenge/situation:

Observations and description:

Recommendations, solutions, and actions:

Results—how did things improve?

Top Ten List of **Program Analyst Accomplishments**

Following are examples of both long and short project descriptions that include the critical skills of a Management Analyst. These projects involve Lean Six Sigma activity studies, studies resulting in new data, test management, research analysis, analysis and solutions to improve a safety program, analysis of post-award contracts, analysis of technical data sets, and process improvement studies.

HISTORICAL LANDSCAPE RESEARCHER/ANALYST, GLEN ECHO PARK. Project Leader/Lead Researcher for Glen Echo Park in Maryland, which was first opened as an educational park in 1891. Glen Echo is a 22-acre National Park Service site currently being used as an amusement park, dance hall, and venue for classes. Objective is to better inform management of assets and resources. Analyzed resources in compliance with Section 110 requirements of the National Historic Preservation Act. The major challenge was being liaison between the Park Service and the nonprofit organization currently renting space at the park for dance events, classes, and children's programs. During the project, consulted on environmental assessment for extending a bike path through the park.

Actions: Organized the information into the format required for the Cultural Landscape Inventory (CLI).

Results: Discovered the Joy Jigger ride, an original patent, as well as 20 other previously unseen amusement park patents. Produced a 100-page report, which includes photographs, text, archival drawings, maps, chronology of dates, and patent index. I made recommendations on several significant issues of historic integrity and contributions to the local cultural landscape.

ANALYZED AND MANAGED COMMUNICATIONS CONTRACT—SAVED MONEY.
Chaired a Sole Source Selection Board for a three-year communications contract worth $3 million. I led the board in setting the policies for all ongoing advertising, brand identity, marketing programs, and evaluating effectiveness of advertising, outreach, and communication marketing and contract staffing. When I became the chairman, four vendors were known to be interested in the contract, but I felt that their skills and professionalism levels would not meet our objectives. I requested changes in the statement of work and reductions in the contract fees. We use a large amount of communication resources, social media/web/print/exhibits, and we needed the required skill sets from the contractors.

I drafted and evaluated the contract procedures. I directed the cross-disciplinary team in evaluation of the proposal.

Results: I was instrumental in a 65% reduction in our contract costs by identifying new contract skills and recommending new techniques for improving the processes of communications contractors.

TEST MANAGER FOR DEFENSE TRAVEL SYSTEM—DEVELOPED MORE EFFICIENT SYSTEMS. Test Manager for Defense Travel System, an enterprise automated travel management system first established in 2007 throughout DOD with more than 2 million DOD users worldwide. I consult with managers concerning staff performance, reports, and customer services. Log and track major problems to ensure that solutions were implemented and information was disseminated quickly to users. Oversee and direct 15 testing contractors managing the updates, programming, and researching problems. The challenges are that the updates are monthly and new problems appear with each update.

Results: As a result of close logging and tracking problems, errors were reduced from 15,000 logged errors in 2007 when the system was new, to 1,234 errors logged in 2010. Dramatically improved efficient updating of the software with no time down for updates.

EVALUATE SOLUTIONS TO IMPROVE CONTRACTOR SAFETY PROGRAM. As Team Leader, tasked to evaluate and develop solutions for common issues to drive the improvement of a contractor safety program; organized multidisciplinary teams to identify and address key safety issues with contractors and the onsite staff. Developed and presented a training program to increase the awareness of safety in areas where metrics showed an increase in repeated incidents.

Results: Reduced recordable events by 23% at sites where the training program had been implemented. The results drove an acceptance-to-apply process by other project teams.

QUANTITATIVE AND QUALITATIVE ANALYSIS: Managed six Ph.D. AT&T Bell Labs technical staff members in the analytical techniques and tools needed to evaluate data sets on international telecommunication technology and usage patterns for base protection and market-share-growth activities. Applied analytical and evaluative methods and techniques for assessing program and project development or execution, and improving organizational effectiveness and efficiency. Employed understanding of strategic planning and product management principles and techniques. Applied fact-finding and investigative techniques. Led data analysis efforts to categorize client base and create programs matching client base need. Provided technical sales and account management services. Performed simple and complex network designs, recommendations, and proposals.

Results: Instrumental in the negotiation and agreement of a Nabisco National Letter of Agency for utilizing only AT&T for all long-distance services for the entire company.

LEAN PROCESS IMPROVEMENTS. Implemented Lean process improvement methods that significantly reduced project costs, lowered staff resource requirements, and thus improved the project management process and performance results. Projects under my control have included construction and supervising the work of professional/technical personnel assigned to projects. Completed project scope, schedules, and cost estimates and provided professional engineering expertise on technical areas and design changes. Applied engineering skills, knowledge, and abilities in project design, construction, geotechnical, and environmental areas.

Results: Identified and completed several Lean Energy projects to achieve the cost savings of $650K at a pilot facility. This resulted in adding drive to the projects' sustainability.

IMPLEMENTED CHANGE TO IMPROVE CUSTOMER SERVICES that positively impacted design of the employee Call Center, employee on-boarding/off-boarding processes, and background check review. Analyzed and updated domestic and international relocation processes.

CONDUCTED STUDIES; DEVELOPED AND MONITORED THE EXECUTION AND REPORTING OF PERFORMANCE DATA for strategic HC and HR projects and initiatives. Applied knowledge of analytical tools and techniques to analyze and evaluate effectiveness; recommended improvements.

US 1-9 COMPLIANCE AND AUDIT. Spearheaded automation of I-9 Employment Verification form through E-Verify, which streamlined the process and ensured compliance with federal regulations and contract requirements.

PROMOTED SMART CARD TECHNOLOGY to improve the effectiveness and efficiency of agency-wide business activities. Created the business case, working capital fund justification, program management plan, governance framework, and charter for the Smart Card Program Management Office.

Keywords and Skills for **Three Occupational Series**

While the following occupational series seem very different, they actually contain similar skills and responsibilities that you can translate into your Management and Program Analyst resume.

Administrative Management/Policy, 0301

- Skill in presenting information and negotiating resolutions
- Ability to analyze and evaluate complex issues
- Knowledge of budgetary principles, practices, laws, and regulations
- Ability to lead and direct others

Management and Program Analysis, 0343

- Development of long-range goals, objectives, strategies, and multilayered transition implementation plans
- Application of analytical and evaluative methods and techniques to assess program development
- Estimates lifecycle/cost-benefit analysis of projects and analyzes the economic impact on programs
- Leads cost-effectiveness studies across coordinating centers' operations and administrative programs

Medical and Health, 0601

- The Medical Center Director has overall responsibility for planning, organizing, directing, coordinating, and controlling medical, administrative, and supporting operations of a healthcare facility
- Administers medical care and treatment, or a consolidated medical and veterans' benefits facility for a large geographic area
- Develops and implements a comprehensive health-care delivery system tailored to the needs of the veteran patient population served
- Establishes and maintains effective and harmonious relationships with local communities; veterans' organizations; civic, professional, and other similar organizations; and with other hospitals

Final Tips for **Writing Your Resume**

Research the Mission of the Office or Agency

Considering the mission of the office or agency will help you write a more compelling resume. Research the challenges of the agency or office to consider its analysis and project priorities. For instance, if you are applying to FEMA, you should know that problem solving, efficient operations, and working under pressure are critical competencies. If you are applying to TSA, think about your experience with fast-changing priorities, media reports, emergencies, and threats.

Add the Numbers and Quantify Your Information

In order to write a "quantitatively correct" Management Analyst resume, you will need numbers to demonstrate that you can track information, demonstrate results, prove performance and efficiency, and present data. Because Management Analysis is all about information management, your resume should demonstrate these skills at the basic resume writing level.

How Does Your Private-Sector Job Involve Management Analyst Skills?

Just because your private-industry job title is not "Management Analyst" does not mean you can't qualify for a Management Analyst position in the federal government. The following are private-sector occupations that match the public-sector Management and Program Analyst job:

- Advertising Director
- Business Analyst
- Business Process Engineer
- Category Analyst
- Configuration Analyst
- Database Administrator
- Marketing Analyst, Market Researcher
- Operations Manager
- Program Analyst
- Program Manager
- Programmer Analyst (play down the IT part of your work)
- Project Manager
- Quality Systems Administrator
- Research Analyst
- Sales Executive (focus on marketing, analysis, and program management)
- Strategic Analyst
- Systems Analyst
- Web Project Engineer
- Writer-Editor

MANAGEMENT AND PROGRAM ANALYST, GS-0343-13   02/2011 to 07/2015
Commander, Navy Installations Command (CNIC)   40 Hours per Week
Washington Navy Yard, Washington, DC 20374
Supervisor: CDR David Smith, 202-444-4444, may contact

ANALYZED FINANCIAL, CIVILIAN, AND MILITARY MANPOWER RESOURCES for four U.S. Navy installations: US Navy Pay Transient Personnel Units (TPUs); Shore Corrections/Regional Restricted Barracks; Pretrial Confinement Facilities (PCFs); and Detention Facilities (DETFACs) worldwide. Developed annual business and execution plans aligned with the strategic plan, to assure support for the development of the Total Force Strategy for the Shore Corrections and TPU.

ADMINISTERED MULTIMILLION DOLLAR PROGRAM BUDGETS. Developed, tracked, and managed a $5M budget for the Navy Mobilization Processing Sites (NMPS) program for FY-13. Created annual spend plan for labor/non-labor, tracked program execution rates, notified leadership of critical budget shortfalls, and justified funding. Managed a $6M+ annual program budget for the Transient Personnel Branch. Managed a $2.5M Entitlement Travel Program budget covering military and civilian personnel and dependents.

USED AUTOMATED AND WEB-BASED FINANCIAL SYSTEMS to track, manage, and monitor resource planning, financial administration, and budget formulation and execution. Trusted subject matter expert (SME) in the use of the Command Financial Management System (CFMS) system and go-to person for assistance with CFMS reports and funds verifications. Created and maintained customized financial tracking tools to monitor current expenditures, remaining balances, and allocations for budget tasking and data calls.

CONTRACTING OFFICER REPRESENTATIVE (COR): Managed and executed accurate funding execution for four government contracts valued in excess of $1.9M. Reviewed proposals and recommended selections to Contracting Officer. Submitted contracting packages for sole source funding and option year execution. Wrote Statement of Work (SOW) for new solicitations and ensured solicitations were compliant with regulations. Approved invoice payments. Worked with vendors to rectify discrepancies. Contractor Verification System (CVS) representative for N1.

KEY ACCOMPLISHMENTS:
- Developed and led process improvements that reduced contract and manpower costs across the enterprise. Initiated an 8% budget cut and guided all regions in more stringent enforcement of entitlement travel expenditures.
- Through effective financial management, astute analysis of baseline program requirements, and cost reduction strategies, successful in reducing the $5.4M POM 2014 budget to $4.1M. Identified "must fund" items, replaced personnel support contracts with military manpower, and developed a POM Capability Plan.
- Created a customized financial tracking tool that provided leadership with a snapshot of current expenditures, remaining balances, and allocated controls; and improved budget administration.
- Developed business case analysis; led team in formulating data to support drawdown planning and facilities closure. Presented recommendations to senior leadership that resulted in a $5M in cost savings over two years.

SPECIAL TOPIC Career Change Resumes

Have you been in the same position for over five years, and are you ready for a change? If you are a current federal employee, are you trying to change your job series? If you are a private industry jobseeker, are you trying to change your position or career to enter the government? If you are one of these people, then you need a "career change resume," and this chapter is for you.

Changing careers and occupational series in government is challenging, because the resume has to show the qualifications and the "one year specialized experience" in the new area of work. Sometimes you can change your job series with education, but most of the time, the announcements will state that you have to show the one year specialized experience.

Making a "career change" within the federal government requires additional care to prepare a resume to compete against other applicants who have already been on that track and may be more qualified than you. Even a change within the same occupational series and same agency can be considered a career change if the job duties and responsibilities are different enough. This chapter will help you translate your current competencies, knowledge, skills, and abilities into a new occupational series, or a very different job within your current series.

We will give you some tips and ideas for preparing your career change resume, and we will show you two sample career changes to see how it's done, as well as one successful career change resume:

- ❯ **Case Study 1:** IRS Revenue Agent, GS 7 to USCIS Immigration Assistant, GS-6
- ❯ **Case Study 2:** Administrative Officer, GS-0341-12 to Program Analyst, GS-0340-13
- ❯ **Successful Resume:** Tax Examining Technician, IRS, GS-7 to Immigration Analyst Assistant, DHS, GS-7

Most career change objectives focus on achieving a higher grade level or more/ different challenges in the federal career. For example:

- IRS Revenue Agent (GS-7) to any other kind of Agent with any other agency (GS-7/9)

- Administrative Assistant (GS-9) to Administrative Specialist (GS-11)

- Administrative Specialist/Administrative Officer GS-11/12 to Program Analyst (GS-12/13)

- Program Analyst (GS-11/12) to Contract Specialist (GS-12/13)

- Contract Specialist (GS-9/11) to Grants Management Specialist (GS-12) or vice versa

- IT Specialist (Customer Services/Systems Admin) to Quality Assurance Specialist

- Park Ranger (GS-5/7/9) to Interpreter (GS-7/9/11)

- Maintenance Worker (WG-8) to Electronic Technician (GS-9/11)

- Maintenance Worker (WG-10) to Facilities Specialist (GS-11)

- Agriculture Marketing Specialist (GS-11/12) to Contract Specialist (GS-12/13)

- Program Analyst (GS-13) to Program Manager (GS-14)

Is Your Career Change Even Possible?

To be Eligible for a position:
You must be able to demonstrate that you have the required "one year specialized experience" listed in the vacancy announcement.

To be Best Qualified and Referred:
You must also have all or most of the knowledge, skills, and abilities (KSAs) outlined in the vacancy announcement. Your resume must include keywords from the announcement, and your questionnaire must be answered at the highest level.

To be Interviewed:
You must include accomplishments to demonstrate your transferable skills and competencies that are required for the new target position and to convince the hiring manager that you are the best candidate for the position.

Comparing Keywords for the **Outline Format Resume**

These career changes could work!

CURRENT Position Keywords

TARGET Position Keywords

ADMINISTRATIVE OFFICER, GS-0341-12

- Maintain administrative operations
- Manage and study space and facilities
- Improve operations efficiency
- Prepare reports on program needs
- Prepare reports, including statistical analysis
- Monitor work of administratie staff
- Recommend process improvements
- Provide budget updates and finance advice
- Prepare and present proposals
- Communicate with staff

MANAGEMENT ANALYST (QUALITY), GS-0343-13

- Manage studies
- Quality improvement projects
- Maintain files and document trends
- Analyze program needs
- Prepare statistical analysis
- Lead process improvements
- Recommend policies
- Lean methodologies or similar
- Communications and briefings

LOGISTICS MANAGEMENT SPECIALIST, SV-0346-I/J2

- Plan, coordinate, and evaluate logistics
- Implement logistics support strategies
- Ensure effectiveness and efficiency of operations
- Identify specific requirements for operations
- Knowledge of operational concepts
- Collaborate with contractors
- Analyze acquisition options
- Contracting officer representative
- Technical monitor–logistics suport contracts

ADMINISTRATIVE OFFICER, GS-0341-12

- Maintain administrative operations
- Manage and study space and facilities
- Improve operations efficiency
- Prepare reports on program needs
- Prepare reports, including statistical analysis
- Monitor work of administrative staff
- Recommend process improvements
- Provide budget updates and finance advice
- Prepare and present proposals
- Communicate with staff

IRS TAX EXAMINING TECHNICIAN, GS-059-07

- Research and resolve tax account issues
- Communicate daily, orally and in writing with taxpayers
- Draw on accounting, financial analysis, and decision-making skills
- Perform complex financial transactions; determine penalties and interest
- Apply knowledge of individual and business tax law
- Financial analysis project
- Pilot program team
- Training lead
- Excel team
- Employee satisfaction team
- Selected as workgroup leader

USCIS IMMIGRATION SERVICES ASSISTANT, GS-1802-6

- Research, analyze and compile data
- Direct service to customers
- Pre-screen applications
- Provide routine information regarding immigration
- Review and screening of applications for benefits
- Analyze data
- Complex office automation
- Maintain operating procedures
- Manage and organize information
- Oral and written communications

8 Steps to Career Change in Government

1. Find a target announcement for the grade level and occupational series you are seeking. Look for announcements listing the transferable skills that you possess, and avoid the announcements that require specialized knowledge or skills that you do not currently have.

2. Analyze the specialized experience, KSAs, and Questionnaire.

3. Make sure you have the "one year specialized experience" from your last position or a previous position within the last ten years.

4. Make sure that you can answer the questionnaire at a high level.

5. Make a list of new keywords.

6. Update or revise your outline format federal resume with the new words.

7. Write an accomplishment that proves your highest level and most complex experiences. If possible, add three to five accomplishments to stand out even more.

8. Prepare longer accomplishment stories for your interview.

Treat the resume like a response to a
Request for Proposal (RFP)

Each RFP is different, and a vendor must make sure to address every requirement carefully when preparing a response to an RFP in order to qualify. A federal resume is much the same; every requirement from the vacancy announcement should be addressed diligently in your resume.

What You Must Do to Succeed

Basically, everything you have learned in Part 1 of this book still applies, just more so. The career change resume can be a challenge, but it is possible!

One Resume Does Not Fit All: You must tweak your resume for each and every application to show that you are qualified for that particular position. Every announcement will have different requirements and those requirements must be demonstrated in your resume.

One Year Specialized Experience: In your resume, you must address how you meet the "one year specialized experience" listed in the vacancy announcement. Include the dates for your work experience in order to get the one-year time credit for your experience. This information is critical!

KSAs: The KSAs from the announcement must also be demonstrated in your resume. Analyze them carefully, and if you have a particular KSA, include it in your resume. To get referred and selected for an interview, add accomplishments that will demonstrate your past performance with these KSAs.

Transferable skills: Highlight the skills that you have that can be transferred to the new position, such as oral or written communication skills.

Keywords: Find the keywords in the vacancy announcement and use them as your paragraph headers in your Outline Format federal resume (see Part 1 of this book for how to prepare a resume in the Outline Format).

Accomplishments: Include noteworthy accomplishments to show that you can do your job well, and that you have skills your future employer will want to have on board. Make sure to have at least one accomplishment on the first page of your resume. For career and occupational change, accomplishments are critical to get referred and invited to an interview.

Questionnaire: The Questionnaire is a test, and generally you must have a score of at least 90% to be referred to the supervisor. Give yourself all of the credit that you can on each and every question.

Factor Evaluation System (FES): Use the Factor Evaluation System descriptions found in the Occupational Standards to improve your resume. The FES contains wording to help you demonstrate higher levels of performance in your resume.

Using the FES to Improve Your Career Change Resume

Where to Find the FES

The FES can be found in the Position Classification Standards for your series (if they are available). Visit https://www.opm.gov/policy-data-oversight/classification-qualifications/classifying-general-schedule-positions/#url=Standards. Sometimes they are called Factor Level Descriptions.

The FES Factors

❯ **Knowledge Required by the Position:** What knowledge do you have to help you do your job?

❯ **Supervisory Controls:** Who are you in charge of? Are you independent?

❯ **Guidelines:** What laws or regulations are you an expert in? May include Legislation, Manuals, SOP, Policies, References

❯ **Complexity:** How complicated is your job?

❯ **Scope & Effect:** Who do you talk to and work with? What is the scope of your work? Is it local, regional, worldwide?

❯ **Personal Contacts and Purpose of Contacts:** Who are your customers? Are they nearby or do you work with them through email, etc.? How many customers do you support? Are they local? Global?

Using the Descriptions

The FES gives clear definitions for each factor corresponding with each GS level.

For example, for the Environmental Protection Specialist, the level of SUPERVISORY CONTROL expected at about the GS-9/11 level is described as: "The supervisor outlines assignment objectives, priorities, and deadlines and provides advice on how to proceed when unusual problems are encountered that cannot be resolved by application of clear precedents."

At the GS-14 level, this would be expected: "As a recognized authority in a program or functional area, the Environmental Protection Specialist has complete responsibility and authority to plan, design, schedule, and carry out major programs, projects, studies, or other work independently."

These descriptions are what the Human Resources Specialists use to determine what level you are performing at in your position. You can use these descriptions to help you clarify your performance level.

Example: Sample Resume Excerpt – Before FES

Administrative Assistant (40 hrs per wk) (Massachusetts Air National Guard)
Jan 08 – Present. Provide administrative support to the Chief of Staff (Massachusetts Air National Guard). Provide reports to queries on personnel matters utilizing data systems RCAS and IPERMS. Track Executive Summaries, correspondence, briefings, and investigations utilizing an electronic log system. Review Executive Summaries for content, format, and administrative errors. Maintain Payroll Worksheets for 35 personnel monitoring hours worked and vacations taken, and provide summary reports to supervisors and finance personnel. Manage Moral and Welfare fund requests for Massachusetts National Guard units by reviewing requests for legality, administrative correctness, submitting the paperwork to the State Military Department, and coordinating issuance of checks. Monitor the Chief of Staff's calendar for appointments and events. Assist in developing/mentoring new personnel both enlisted and officer with office procedures.

After FES

We analyzed the Factor Evaluation System for this series, used the FES terminology to clarify the performance level, and added headings to improve readability.

ADMINISTRATIVE ASSISTANT (40 hrs per wk) (Massachusetts Air National Guard)

Assistant to the Chief of Staff who oversees 3,000 Massachusetts National Guard Soldiers. Work independently to support all administrative, personnel, correspondence, and payroll administration for the director.

COMPLEX ADMINISTRATION: Highly skilled in supporting multiple battalion deployments and re-integration and readiness during and following the ending of Iraq and Afghanistan wars.

IMPLEMENT THE NATIONAL GUARD TECHNICIAN HANDBOOK. Implement and administer "The Technician Act of 1968," Public Law 90-486, for all support services for Reserves and Active duty personnel.

REPORTS, DATABASE ADMINISTRATION, AND COMPUTER SKILLS. Produce reports to queries on personnel matters utilizing data systems RCAS and IPERMS. Track suspenses, Executive Summaries, correspondence, briefings, and investigations utilizing an electronic log system.

CUSTOMER SERVICES FOR THE GUARD PERSONNEL: Manage Morale and Welfare fund requests for Massachusetts National Guard units by reviewing requests for legality and administrative correctness; submitting the paperwork to the State Military Department; and coordinating issuance of checks.

ACCOMPLISHMENTS: Improved support for deployed, emergency support for the guardsmen. Organized and coordinated efficient ceremonies and events. Managed paperwork for complex deployments.

Case Study 1: **Career Series Change and Promotion**

Administrative Assistant, GS-0303-9 to Administrative Officer, GS-0341-11

In this case study, the client was an Administrative Assistant (GS-0303-9) and found a vacancy announcement for Administrative Officer (GS-0341-11/12) which was very similar to her current position. If the GS-9 Administrative Assistant has performed all of the tasks of the GS-11 Administrative Officer, then this person COULD demonstrate the "one year specialized experience," change the job series, and get promoted. Let's compare the keywords for each position:

Current Position: Administrative Assistant GS-9

Current Job Description

> **Job Title:** Administrative Staff Assistant, GS-0303-7/8/9
> **Department:** Department Of Transportation
> **Agency:** Federal Railroad Administration
>
> **QUALIFICATIONS FOR THE GS-9:**
> * You must have at least one year of equal or equivalent experience, it must include:
> Experience providing administrative management services to senior level officials to include performing research and preparing reports of various legal and confidential issues.
> * Experience providing administrative/operational advisory services to include travel; correspondence/spreadsheets; time/attendance AND experience interpreting legal regulations and correspondence; conducting research on case files to effectively organize the day to day operations of an office.
> * Experience expressing facts and ideas in writing in a clear, convincing, and organized manner and to make clear and convincing oral and written reports.

Keywords for the Outline Format Federal Resume

- ADMINISTRATIVE MANAGEMENT SERVICES FOR SENIOR LEVEL MANAGERS
- RESEARCH AND PREPARE REPORTS
- ADVISORY SERVICES AND SUPPORT FOR TRAINING AND TRAVEL
- CORRESPONDENCE MANAGEMENT
- RESEARCH CASE FILES
- COMMUNICATE CLEARLY
- COMPUTER AND DATABASE SKILLS

Desired Position: Administrative Officer GS-11/12

Job Title: Administrative Officer
Department: Department Of Homeland Security
Agency: U.S. Secret Service
SALARY RANGE: $58,562.00 to $91,255.00 / Per Year
SERIES & GRADE: GS-0341-11/12

Administrative Officer Specialized Experience, GS 11
GS-11: You qualify for the GS-11 level (starting salary $58,562) if you possess one year of specialized experience equivalent to the GS-09 level performing duties such as: maintaining administrative policies and internal operational procedures for the division; coordinating administrative functions and activities; managing space and facilities; preparing reports; providing financial and budgetary advice; and overseeing, assigning and monitoring the work of administrative support personnel

- Knowledge of the functions, policies, procedures, laws, and regulations pertaining to human resources, finance, budget, procurement, facilities, space acquisition, property, and safety and occupational programs to advise and assist managers with day to day administrative processes.
- Skill in applying federal budget and procurement regulations in order to justify decisions, make recommendations, initiate requests, monitor and track expenditures.
- Ability to direct, advise, and instruct employees concerning administrative operations and procedures.
- Ability to communicate findings, by preparing and presenting proposals and recommendations to various officials, employees and other outside entities.

Keywords for the Outline Format Federal Resume

- ❯ MAINTAIN ADMINISTRATIVE OPERATIONS
- ❯ MANAGE SPACE AND FACILITIES
- ❯ PREPARE REPORTS
- ❯ PROVIDE BUDGET UPDATES AND FINANCE ADVICE
- ❯ MONITOR WORK OF ADMINISTRATIVE STAFF
- ❯ COMMUNICATE WITH STAFF
- ❯ PREPARE AND PRESENT PROPOSALS

Case Study 2: **The GS-12 to GS-13 Challenge**

Administrative Officer GS-0341-12 to Program Analyst GS-0340-13

The promotion objective from GS-12 to GS-13 grade level is challenging and very competitive because of the number of federal employees who have been a GS-12 for 10 or more years. Getting a promotion to GS-13 might take a lot of searching to find announcements that are suitable for you. The announcements for GS-13 can be very specific to the agency mission and KSAs. You will have to find a job announcement that is general enough for you to demonstrate that you do have the "one year specialized experience" in the work of the new target position.

Sample Vacancy Announcement: Management & Program Analyst with Supply Chain Emphasis

This GSA Management & Program Analyst position is about Supply Chain and Supply Transformation. If you do not have "one year specialized experience" in this work, you cannot rate yourself high enough in the questionnaire to get promoted into this position.

Job Title: Management and Program Analyst (0343)
Department: General Services Administration
Agency: Federal Acquisition Service
SALARY RANGE: $90,823.00 to $118,069.00 / Per Year
SERIES & GRADE: GS-0343-13

QUALIFICATIONS REQUIRED:
To qualify, you must demonstrate at least one year of specialized experience equivalent to the GS-12 level in the Federal Service. Specialized experience is experience developing new business processes/models and delivery channels that transform a business portfolio.

Such experience must include knowledge in all of the following:
•   Supply chain management
•   Item management
•   Logistics reassignment
•   Civilian and/or DoD distribution networks
•   Acquisition operations management

Vacancy Questionnaire Questions for which you must answer EXPERT to qualify for the GS-13 position:

From the choices listed below, please select the one that best describes your experience providing management, review and analysis to support supply transformation including maintaining a detailed project plan. [...]

From the choices listed below, please select the one that best describes your experience providing oversight of a risk management plan and mitigation efforts in support of point of sale requirements definition and rollout, managing, upgrading and consolidating infrastructure, establishing new connectivity and sun setting legacy systems in support of supply transformation. [...]

Have you analyzed and evaluated a supply transformation process to ensure compliance with applicable legal, regulatory and policy requirements? Answer to this question is required. [...]

Keywords for the Outline Format Federal Resume

❯ BUSINESS PROCESS ANALYSIS
❯ SUPPLY TRANSFORMATION
❯ PROJECT MANAGEMENT
❯ RISK MANAGEMENT PLAN
❯ EVALUATION OF COMPLIANCE REQUIREMENTS
❯ ACQUISITION OPERATIONS
❯ LOGISTICS MANAGEMENT

Sample Vacancy Announcement: Management and Program Analyst with Quality Assurance Emphasis

Below is a Management and Program Analyst GS-13 position, with an emphasis on process improvement. If you don't have skills in your GS-12 resume that speaks to quality assurance with the language underlined below, then you will probably NOT get best qualified for this GS-13. And to get an interview, you would need examples of process improvement in your GS-12 job description.

Vacancy Announcement Excerpt (keywords in bold)

Job Title: Management and Program Analyst (Quality Assurance)
Department: Department of Homeland Security
Agency: Citizenship and Immigration Services
SALARY RANGE: $90,823.00 to $118,069.00 / Per Year
SERIES & GRADE: GS-0343-13

QUALIFICATIONS REQUIRED:
GS-13: You qualify at the GS-13 level if you possess one (1) year of specialized experience, equivalent to at least the GS-12 level in the federal government, which has equipped you with the skills needed to successfully perform the duties of the position. You must also have experience performing the following duties:

- Preparing and **maintaining files documenting patterns or trends** for use in providing feedback to supervisors and management or to **identify training needs**.
- Planning and **implementing quality improvement projects** to develop, document, and implement effective and **efficient cost saving solutions**.
- **Analyzing program needs, recommending policies and formulating procedures** for local offices and managers.
- Preparing reports regarding **Quality Assurance activities** and accomplishments for submission to appropriate offices

The competencies or knowledge, skills, and abilities needed to perform this job are:
- **PROBLEM SOLVING**
- **COMMUNICATION**
- **PLANNING AND EVALUATING**
- **CUSTOMER SERVICE**
- **ATTENTION TO DETAIL**
- **MANAGEMENT AND PROGRAM ANALYSIS**

Finding Keywords in the **Self-Assessment Questionnaire**

Give yourself all the credit that you can!

The keywords in the following self-assessment questionnaire are in **bold**.

You must provide the position title(s) and dates of employment referenced in your resume that demonstrates the experience related to your response.

For each item, select the ONE response that most accurately describes your current level of experience and capability using the scale below.

A- I have no experience in performing this work activity.

B- I have limited experience in performing this work activity. I have had exposure to this work activity, but would require additional guidance, instruction, or experience to perform it at a proficient level.

C- I have moderate experience performing this work activity for routine or predictable situations with minimal supervision or guidance.

D- I have performed this work activity independently across a wide range of situations. I have assisted others in carrying out this work activity. I seek guidance in carrying out this work activity only in unusually complex situations.

E- I am considered an expert in carrying out this work activity. I have advised and instructed others in carrying out this work activity on a regular basis. I am consulted by my colleagues and/or superiors to carry out this work activity in unusually complex situations.

4. Analyze business processes using **Lean Six Sigma (or equivalent)** methodology and detailed statistical analysis methods to prepare recommendations for efficiencies and cost savings solutions.

5. Develop and **document standard operating procedures**.

6. Develop proposals and promote **effective and efficient execution of local processes**.

7. **Lead process improvement projects**.

8. Coordinate the development, management and communication of an **organization wide quality management program**.

9. Liaise with various internal and external quality offices to **disseminate and improve quality management program** policies and procedures.

10. Coordinate **process improvement projects** across an organization.

11. Plan and develop presentations and information activities which **reflect the critical tasks** performed by an organization and which **address deficiencies, efficiencies, and cost savings**.

12. Using **detailed statistical analysis**, identify, produce, and manage reporting of measures that reflect process performance.

Sample Federal Career Change Resume

Allison Pinter: Current Fed Changes Series and Agencies in Lateral Move

Previous Job Title: Tax Examining Technician, IRS, GS-7
New Job Title: Immigration Analyst Assistant, DHS, GS-7

Project Summary:

Allison was ready to move into a new series, one that offered more opportunity for career advancement. First, we determined the functional skills and qualifications that would be most important to finding a new position in a more analytical role. We focused on the top skills that would be transferable to a new series, including financial analysis, communications, interpreting laws, customer service, and problem solving. We then created a new resume in the Outline Format to better showcase the most important transferable/functional skill sets.

From the Client:

"After six years with the IRS, I was looking for a new job as an analyst. Over the past 10 months, I applied for 12 positions, some of which are still pending in USAJOBS. I was referred to the Selecting Official for three positions. I am happy to report I have accepted a position with DHS as an Immigration Analyst Assistant. Even though the position is a GS-7 and a lateral move, it is in the analyst series and I am confident I will be able to now gain the experience necessary for career advancement. There were four openings and they interviewed 16 people. I have no doubt your resume helped me to land one of those interviews! And, not only did I successfully transition to a new series, my commute is now only 5 minutes; before, it was 30! I plan to contact you again when I am ready to add my new job experience to my resume."

Resume Place Writer: Carla Waskiewicz

ALLISON PINTER
345 Overland Dr.
Sioux Falls, IA 34578

Day Phone: xxx-xxx-xxxx
Evening Phone: xxx-xxx-xxxx
Email: email@gmail.com

SSN: xxx-xx-xxxx
United States Citizen
Veteran's Preference: N/A
Federal Status/Highest Federal Grade: GS-0592-07, Step 3

TAX EXAMINING TECHNICIAN, GS-0592-07, Step 3, 04/2009 to Present
Internal Revenue Service
Sioux Falls, IA 34578
Annual Salary: $41,377; Hours per week: 40
Supervisor: Bob Mills, xxx-xxx-xxxx, permission to contact, yes

OVERVIEW OF IRS EXPERIENCE: Tax Examining Technician, CSCO Division, 0592-07, 4/2009 to Present; Seasonal Tax Examining Technician, Code and Edit Division, 0592-05, 2/2009 to 4/2009; and Customer Service Representative, 0962-05, 10/2007 to 03/2008.

FIVE YEARS OF PROGRESSIVE EXPERIENCE WITH THE IRS providing technical advisement and assistance on tax law and regulations and tax accounting to internal and external customers. Scope of experience includes analyzing confidential taxpayer records and financial condition, advising on tax liability, researching and interpreting complex tax law and regulations in the Internal Revenue Manual (IRM), and setting up financial agreements for taxpayers.

RESEARCH AND RESOLVE TAX ACCOUNT ISSUES: As Tax Examining Technician in the Compliance Services Collection Operations Division (CSCO), respond to and resolve inquiries on a wide range of tax account issues, including delinquency and account adjustments. Provide taxpayers with information and guidance about general service procedures on all types of individual and business accounts for both current and prior year tax rules, regulations, and procedures. Utilize strong organization skills to manage workflow to ensure the most expeditious handling of assigned cases. Utilize the Service Wide Electronic System (SERP) extensively for research.

COMMUNICATE DAILY, ORALLY AND IN WRITING, WITH TAXPAYERS from a wide range of educational, professional, and ethnic backgrounds. Utilize interview techniques to obtain and gather information. Review, respond to, and prepare taxpayer correspondence. Leverage strong interpersonal skills to communicate clearly and effectively with taxpayers about tax return preparation, related schedules and documentation as well as their rights as defined in IRS guidelines.

DRAW ON ACCOUNTING, FINANCIAL ANALYSIS, AND DECISION-MAKING SKILLS to obtain and compile information, analyze facts and resolve tax processing problems. Analyze financial statements to determine the taxpayer's ability to pay. Call taxpayers to gather additional information or discuss available payment options.

PERFORM COMPLEX FINANCIAL TRANSACTIONS; DETERMINE PENALTIES AND INTEREST: Use Decision IA to ensure the adequacy of payment amounts proposed by taxpayers. Utilize advanced functions of the Integrated Data Retrieval System (IDRS) to verify and rectify payment errors and adjust taxpayer accounts. Prepare and issue manual refunds and credit transfers. Compute tax, penalty, and interest, including restricted interest. Independently manage sensitive case problems, which require special handling. Secure payment of delinquent taxes. Recommend lien and/or levy action.

APPLY KNOWLEDGE OF INDIVIDUAL AND BUSINESS TAX LAW, as defined in IRS guidelines, to initiate enforcement and collection actions. Advise taxpayers of options to meet tax obligations. Assist with setting up installment agreements and direct debits using taxpayer's checking account information. Adjust taxpayer accounts to correct payment errors. Review the IRM daily to stay current on updates.

KEY ACCOMPLISHMENTS:
+ FINANCIAL ANALYSIS PROJECT: Selected to test new process to improve program effectiveness. Worked solely on analyzing financial statements to determine if performing one process would increase production rates. Successful in achieving a rate of 1.5 per hour; which beat the previous rate of 1 per hour. Reported statistical results to management.
+ PILOT PROGRAM TEAM: Invited to test trial version of IAT, a suite of tools to improve productivity and research paths on taxpayer accounts. Maintained detailed records of processing issues; provided feedback to developers.
+ TRAINING LEAD: Selected to teach continuing education courses on tax examination after just 18 months on the job. Taught 150 CSCO employees over two years (2011/2012). Created presentation and course materials. In 2012, trained four clerks in three weeks to become tax examining technicians. Prepared all course materials and led training. Also served as the on-the-job instructor. Reviewed the team's work until they became certified. Received two Special Awards for my training leadership.
+ EXCEL TEAM: Volunteered to serve as team liaison for EXCEL meetings. Collected and compiled information from my team about technical issues. Met with tax examiners from departments to review technical issues across the division. Brainstormed solutions, wrote report, and presented recommendations to management to improve customer service and program efficiency.
+ EMPLOYEE SATISFACTION TEAM: Assisted with facilitating monthly departmental meetings to review production goals and share employee process improvement recommendations with management. Served on a subcommittee that developed a website for our department. Analyzed data from the annual employee survey to recommend ways to improve employee job satisfaction.
+ SELECTED AS WORKGROUP LEADER nine times over the past three years.

SEASONAL TAX EXAMINING TECHNICIAN, GS-0592-05, 02/2009 to 04/2009
Internal Revenue Service, Code and Edit Division
Sioux Falls, IA 34578
Annual Salary: $30,772; Hours per week: 40

RESEARCHED, ANALYZED, AND INTERPRETED COMPLEX IRS REGULATIONS AND GUIDELINES: Edited and coded paper tax returns, in accordance with the Internal Revenue Manual (IRM), for forwarding to the data entry department for input to the IRS database. Researched the IRM guidebook, as needed, to confirm specific codes required for editing a return and to stay up to date on changes in IRS guidelines. Prepared and routed tax returns to the appropriate department for further processing.

MONITORED AND MAINTAINED PRODUCTION/PERFORMANCE DATA IN DAILY INVENTORY LOGS: Recorded daily production of cases processed and closed using an Excel spreadsheet for review by the unit supervisor. Tracked workflow progress within the department to ensure production timelines and customer service goals were met. Met weekly with the supervisor and team members to review production statistics for the department, assess efficiency, and processing status.

KEY ACCOMPLISHMENTS:
+ Consistently met or exceeded production and quality goals during 8-week tenure, which ensured taxpayer refunds were issued in a timely manner. Developed tabbing system to quickly access frequently used regulations. Adjusted and prioritized workflow to increase processing efficiency. Accurately processed 300 returns, on average, daily.
+ Assisted other staff with increasing production performance by sharing the IRM manual tabbing method I developed to more quickly reference the guidebook.
+ Offered permanent position as a Tax Examining Technician after 8 weeks on the job.

CUSTOMER SERVICE REPRESENTATIVE, GS-0962-05, 10/2007 to 03/2008
Internal Revenue Service
Sioux Falls, IA 34578
Annual Salary: $29,726; 40 hours per week

PROVIDED EXEMPLARY CUSTOMER SERVICE TO TAXPAYERS: Assisted and advised taxpayers on a wide-range of IRS issues ranging in scope and complexity. Interacted daily with the general public, taxpayers and/or their representatives, tax practitioners, and accountants in a call center environment. Strove to provide clear explanations and instructions to taxpayer questions about refunds, backup withholding, estimated tax payments, when to file returns, tax forms, understanding their responsibilities under the tax code, and other complex issues. Provided information on how to request abatement of penalties and interest. Responded to as many as 20 calls per day.

UTILIZED INTERVIEW TECHNIQUES TO GATHER TAXPAYER INFORMATION: Conducted telephone interviews with taxpayers and their representatives. Used both targeted interview questions and strong listening skills to gather and assimilate information quickly, often under sensitive conditions.
+ Achieved a perfect record of five (out of five) on random call quality reviews of recorded customer interface calls.

DEMONSTRATED STRONG CONFLICT RESOLUTION AND INTERPERSONAL SKILLS in dealing with difficult people. Fielded calls from frustrated and sometimes irate customers. Strove to remain polite, professional, and calm at all times. Successful in diffusing tense situations.
+ By being patient, methodical, and professional I was successful in resolving an ongoing customer service/processing issue for a man and his son, who both had the same name. Although the customer started out very angry, despite being on an extended hold while I researched and corrected the issue, at the conclusion of the call he thanked me for my dedication to resolving the problem.

RESEARCHED CONFIDENTIAL RECORDS IN IRS SYSTEMS; EXPLAINED IRS REGULATIONS: Researched the Integrated Data Retrieval System (IDRS), the IRS database system used to manage all taxpayer data to find answers to taxpayer questions. Responded to a variety of tax law questions and issues. Reviewed forms, notices, and updates to tax code and regulations, daily, to stay up to date on frequent legislative changes or administrative determinations affecting policy. Also used SERP extensively for research.

DREW ON STRONG DECISION-MAKING SKILLS to provide expert advice to customers as expeditiously as possible, based on the information ascertained in those sources. Cross-referenced records, as needed, to verify joint accounts or other tax relationships. Executed command codes to initiate accurate credit transfers and installment agreements for taxpayers.

LEVERAGED ACCOUNTING EXPERTISE AND KNOWLEDGE OF QUANTITATIVE/QUALITATIVE TECHNIQUES to assemble and analyze balances due on a taxpayer's account and to assist customers with determining the monthly payments. This was often a complex process that involved analysis of multiple years of taxes to devise and recommend a solution. Initiated command codes to input verbal installment agreement into our computer system, IDRS.
+ Completed "Balance Due Training" to become proficient in setting up a complex IRS Installment Agreement repayment program.

OFFICE MANAGER, 9/2001 to 9/2007
Panding Law Office
Sioux Falls, IA 34578
Annual Salary: $45,000; 40 hours per week
Supervisor: Lisa Yellin, xxx-xxx-xxxx, may contact

PLANNED AND COORDINATED DAILY OFFICE OPERATIONS for a small law firm in Sioux Falls, Iowa, with one attorney and two support staff. Performed a wide range of administrative and legal assistance support functions to ensure the smooth and efficient operation of the office. Scope of work included legal research, legal document preparation and management, scheduling/calendar management, electronic/paper files management, correspondence, confidential client records, supply procurement/inventories, billing/invoices, payroll, and special research projects.

PLANNED, COORDINATED, AND ESTABLISHED PROCEDURES AND TIMELINES FOR PROJECTS to ensure effective case management and to ensure all supporting documentation was delivered by deadlines. Managed multiple, concurrent projects. Prioritized and realigned schedules based on changing parameters and deadlines. Troubleshot and resolved administrative issues. Initiated changes to improve productivity, work efficiencies, and operations. Meticulously supervised the flow of a high volume of incoming and outgoing mail, fax communications, and other paperwork. Developed and maintained a follow-up calendar for over 500 active files.

PREPARED, EDITED, AND COMPILED COMPLEX LEGAL CORRESPONDENCE AND TECHNICAL DOCUMENTS including briefs, letters of intent, replies, affidavits, client letters, and memoranda. Prepared and performed filings with courts and government agencies.

PERFORMED LEGAL RESEARCH AND ANALYSIS; MAINTAINED CONFIDENTIAL CLIENT RECORDS: Researched and analyzed continual changes in case law using FindLaw. Researched in-house databases and electronic information retrieval systems, such as LexisNexis, Westlaw, and Video Evidence, to provide attorneys with critical facts for their cases. Sorted and classified data. Maintained historical files and electronic databases.

COMMUNICATED DAILY, orally and in writing, with attorney, staff, clients, court personnel, and other business professionals. Fielded inquiries by phone and in-person from potential clients. Ensured the highest levels of service to customers. Planned, organized, and facilitated meetings for law firm staff to disseminate case law updates, orally and in writing, and to ensure all staff stayed abreast of changes.

MANAGED BILLING, PAYROLL, FINANCIAL ACCOUNTS, PERSONNEL DOCUMENTS: Processed incoming payments, prepared daily bank deposits, and reconciled accounts. Prepared monthly client charges and summary reports for use in long- and short-range planning. Troubleshot and resolved billing issues. Filed quarterly employment tax reports and payments.

DEMONSTRATED KNOWLEDGE OF INTERVIEW TECHNIQUES to obtain and gather information from clients, vendors, attorneys, and other business professionals. Recruited, interviewed, and hired new support staff.

IMPROVED THE EFFECTIVENESS AND EFFICIENCY OF OPERATIONS: Developed customized Excel spreadsheets to automate financial and administrative functions previously done manually. The new computerized records system improved productivity and reduced financial errors. I also set up WiFi to network computers and printers throughout the office.

EDUCATION

B.S. in Criminal Justice/Minor in Business

University of Iowa, School of Law, 2000-2001
Completed 15 credit hours in Graduate Level Law Courses

COURSEWORK, LICENSURES, AND CERTIFICATIONS

UNDERGRADUATE COURSES included: Principles of Finance, Principles of Economics, Principles of Managerial Accounting, and the Legal Environment of Business.

PROFESSIONAL TRAINING

INTERNAL REVENUE SERVICE: Financial Analysis, 12/2009; CSCO New Hire Training, 6/2009; Code and Edit/New Hire Training, 2/2009; CSR New Hire Training, 10/2007; CSR Balance Due Training, 2/2008.

AFFILIATIONS

National Treasury Employment Association Union

ADDITIONAL INFORMATION

SUMMARY OF QUALIFICATIONS

Top performing, personable TAX EXAMINING TECHNICIAN with five years of progressive experience with the Internal Revenue Service (IRS) delivering technical advisement, tax accounting educational assistance, and customer service to individual and business taxpayers. Scope of experience includes analyzing confidential taxpayer records and financial conditions, advising on tax liability, and researching and interpreting complex tax law and regulations in the Internal Revenue Manual (IRM). Integral member of process improvement teams. Valued throughout career for exceptional customer interface, organization and time management skills. Outstanding record of performance, reliability, confidentiality, and high ethical standards. Nine years of real estate sales and law firm experience, including staff

EXPERTISE INCLUDES:

+ Excellent qualifications examining taxpayer returns to determine federal tax liabilities and ensure compliance with the Internal Revenue Code.

+ Strong accounting and financial analysis skills gained through work experience, education, and training. Skilled in the analysis of a taxpayer's financial condition and related operations.

+ Excel in the research and analysis of complex tax issues, financial statements, and accounting records.

+ Internal training lead for Tax Examination courses and other continuing education including "Dealing with Difficult People."

+ Proven ability to contribute as a team player and interface effectively with customers, staff, and senior management. Excellent oral and written communication skills.

+ Comprehensive knowledge of Internal Revenue Code. Familiar with Generally Accepted Accounting Principles (GAAP).

+ Proficient in using MS Office and IRS database systems and software including SERP and IDRS.

COMPUTER SKILLS: Microsoft Office (Word, Excel, Access, PowerPoint, Outlook), FrontPage, Publisher, QuickBooks, Integrated Data Retrieval System (IDRS), Service Wide Electronic System (SERP), FindLaw, Westlaw, and LexisNexis. Type 40 words per minute. HTML coding experience.

HONORS AND AWARDS

Performance Awards, 2012, 2011
Special Awards, Internal Revenue Service, 2012 (2)
Top Listing Agent 07/2006; 09/2006; Top Overall Sales, 02/2006; 04/2006

Get More Expert Help With Your Federal Application!

The Resume Place Senior Executive Services Writers and Consultants are experts at preparing a federal resume to help you compete for the highy-prized federal positions.

Our services:

- Federal Resume Writing in the format preferred by Human Resources Specialists and Hiring Managers

- Federal Career Coaching

- Senior Executive Service Application Preparation

- Interview Prep

- And more!

More Information:

www.resume-place.com

(888) 480-8265

Free Federal Career Info!

Visit www.resume-place.com for:

- Free webinars about federal resume and federal career consulting services

- Free webinars on Hiring Reform and how it will affect your federal job search

- Free KSA, Federal Resume, and Cover Letter Builders

- Up-to-the minute federal job search info—register for our informative newsletter

- Federal job search news articles, updated daily

From the Foreword to the Federal Resume Guidebook, 5th Edition:

"So – what's the savvy job applicant to do? Clearly, they will need to do their homework and pay close attention to the relevant details about the job and the application process contained in the announcement for each federal job in which they are interested. Simply submitting the same boiler-plate resume and cover letter to every job one sees is not going to be nearly as successful as a carefully tailored response that speaks to the specifics of each job.

... **Kathryn Troutman** has literally made a career out of understanding and tracking the evolution of the federal hiring system and translating that understanding into practical advice for the job seeker."

John Palguta
Vice President of Policy
Partnership for Public Service